SOUTHERN NILOTIC HISTORY

SOUTHERN NILOTIC HISTORY

*Linguistic Approaches
to the Study of the Past*

CHRISTOPHER EHRET

NORTHWESTERN UNIVERSITY PRESS
EVANSTON, ILLINOIS
1971

CHRISTOPHER EHRET

is Assistant Professor of History

at the University of California at Los Angeles

CONTENTS

LIST OF APPENDIXES

List of Maps

List of Figures

ix

PREFACE

Southern Nilotic history, like the history of many other African peoples, lacks documents or historical traditions for all but the most recent centuries. It hardly needs reiterating that the historian has numerous other kinds of evidence on which he can draw. Yet such evidence has previously been utilized in so unsystematic and uncoordinated a fashion that the gain in our knowledge of African history through these means has been disappointingly small in quantity and distressingly poor in quality. This study of Southern Nilotic history is therefore of necessity not only an investigation of the events of that history but an essay in the development of a methodology for reconstructing other histories of this kind.

As a history, the study for the most part breaks new ground. There are often no earlier views either to support or attack. For example, the prominent role of Southern Cushites in the development of the Southern Nilotes has simply never been noticed, although there has been some evidence available from which to infer this role. Many other significant developments have been missed, on the other hand, because the relevant evidence had never been collected.

While remaining unaware of most aspects of Southern Nilotic history, would-be historians of ancient East Africa have been curiously preoccupied with one broad topic bearing on that history, namely, the nature of Eastern Cushitic—that is, "Hamitic"—influences on the Southern Nilotes and other East African peoples. The present study assumes a view at odds with the major earlier view on these matters, which classed the Southern and Eastern Nilotes together as "Nilo-Hamites" by reason of their supposed common origin as people of mixed Hamitic and Nilotic ancestry. But this view rested on the indiscriminate association of all evidence which at all pointed to Cushitic influence. A more discriminating analysis of the evidence suggests that the Southern Nilotes were influenced by an Eastern Cushitic people independently from the Eastern Nilotes, that Eastern Cushites influenced the Southern Nilotes far more strongly than they ever influenced the Eastern Nilotes, and that, not only did Eastern Cushites influence Nilotes, but Nilotes at times influenced Eastern Cushites.

Contrary to the view put forward recently by G. P. Murdock,[1] there is no reason at present to postulate any significant "Megalithic" Eastern Cushitic population in southern and central Kenya and bordering areas of Tanzania before the entrance of the Bantu and the Southern Nilotes into the region. Linguistic evidence for such a population is lacking, and the mixed bag of "Cushitic" culture traits among Southern Nilotes and Bantu on which Murdock bases his proposal can best be seen as deriving variously from the influences of Southern Cushites, who certainly preceded the Bantu and Southern Nilotes through large areas of Kenya and Tanzania, and of Southern Nilotes, who brought from the north culture traits which they themselves had originally adopted under Eastern Cushitic influence.

This history of the Southern Nilotes also parts ways with Murdock on at least one other significant point. Murdock considers the development of habits of intensive cattle-keeping among East African peoples to be no more than about a thousand years old. The present study requires that intensive cattle-keeping practices date from at least two thousand years ago, and probably much earlier, in eastern Africa and that the simple keeping of livestock goes back another two or three thousand years before that.

As an essay in methodology, the study is not so much a new thing as a new approach to old things. Most of the particular techniques of investigation have been known for a long time. What is different here is that these techniques have been combined and coordinated by a historian, with the interests and biases of a historian, for the purpose of writing nothing less than history. To the extent that the approach is new, the study only initiates the discussion of a methodology which will begin to take more nearly final form as it is tempered in the fire of continuing research and debate. Some of the presuppositions, for instance, which inform the interpretation of evidence cannot yet be claimed to have application outside the context of East African, and especially Southern Nilotic, cultures and events. More important, not all the techniques which should make up the methodology have been utilized in the study. In particular, the kinds of evidence provided by archaeology and place-name study, areas of investigation where work is only just beginning for East Africa, must eventually be correlated with the kinds of evidence used here. For example, while relative dating is easily set up, the establishment of a firm absolute chronology of Southern Nilotic history will depend on the discovery of

1. *Africa: Its Peoples and Their Culture History* (New York: McGraw-Hill Book Co., Inc., 1959).

correlatable archaeological evidence. The dating suggested in Chapter 3 cannot be more than a vague approximation of the likely times of particular developments; it is presented in lieu of better evidence and to assist the eventual identification of archaeological cultures with peoples in this history.

The kind of approach to Southern Nilotic history worked out here is not an exotic effort, possible only because of some peculiar characteristics of the Southern Nilotic past. The writer could just as well have written a history, of similar depth and detail, of the Eastern Nilotes or of the Southern Cushites; and without a doubt the whole of sub-Saharan Africa abounds in possible topics for this kind of history. Indeed, without some such historical methodology as that used here to investigate Southern Nilotic history, historians can hardly hope ever to know more than the barest outline of Africa's earlier history.

CHRISTOPHER EHRET

Los Angeles
November, 1969

ACKNOWLEDGMENTS

It goes without saying that many people have contributed in varied ways to this work. For the fellowship support which made the study possible as a whole I am indebted to the Foreign Area Fellowship Program. I am grateful also to Professor Jack Berry for his tutelage and encouragement, to the history department at Northwestern University for allowing me to pursue an unusual type of historical research, to Mrs. Susie Wood for preparing the original manuscript of this book, and to Professor Jan Vansina for reading and criticizing the earlier draft.

A large part of the actual collection of evidence for the book was carried out in East Africa, and so I wish to express my especial thanks to the governments of Kenya and Tanzania, to all the East Africans whose hospitality, friendship, and interest made my wife's and my stay one we will always remember with happiness, and to the University College, Nairobi, and the University College, Dar es Salaam, which together provided me with an academic home during the period of my research in East Africa. I am particularly grateful to Professor B. A. Ogot of the history department at the University College, Nairobi, for his support and encouragement. Of the many other East Africans to whom I am indebted I must give special mention to Messrs. Afraim Hayuma, Servitus Malai, Francis Kigen, Henry Mwambu, and Mwangi Macharia.

I owe special thanks also to John Sutton, Tom Gorman, whose typewriter I used in Nairobi, Professor A. N. Tucker, Gilbert Asher, who helped us in so many ways when we first arrived in East Africa, Professor Franklin Scott, Professor Oswald Werner, and Dr. Peter Cox and his family and the several others who gave of both their help and their hospitality.

C. E.

Southern Nilotic History

CHAPTER 1

Introduction

THE PEOPLE

A people's history does not begin with their memories. It begins rather with their emergence as a separate group. If their emergence and early development lie beyond the reach of the historian's familiar source, human memory as it appears in documents and oral traditions, the historian cannot therefore say that such events are darkness and not history. But he should also, and legitimately as a historian, utilize whatever sources he can to penetrate the darkness and reveal it as history. It would be a different kind of history. It would not name individual leaders, or describe particular wars, or encompass its events with precise dates. But it would nevertheless be a history of population movement, cultural change and interchange, and technological development. The history of the Southern Nilotic peoples of East Africa in the eras preceding the 1600's must be this kind of history.

The modern Southern Nilotes[1] live mainly in Kenya and Tanzania. They fall linguistically into two major groups: the Dadog[2] of southern Mbulu Area and other nearby country in Tanzania (see Map 1), and the Kalenjin of western Kenya, some of whom extend also slightly into Uganda just north of Mount Elgon (see Map 2).

The Dadog consist of several subtribes, often speaking their own dialects of the Dadog language. The largest of these groups is the Barabaig; perhaps 15,000 or more in number, they inhabit the plains south of Mount Hanang in southern Mbulu area, Tanzania. Other subtribes are the Gisamjeng, who live just north of the Barabaig; the Iseimajeg and Rudageing of the Ruwana Valley of Musoma area; the Buradig, Bajud, and Dororajeg of the plains running

---

1. An alternate name, the Highland Nilotes, has recently been coined to denote the peoples here called Southern Nilotes; the alternative name has been used notably in B. A. Ogot and J. Kieran (eds.), *Zamani: A Survey of East African History* (Nairobi: Longmans and East African Publishing House, 1968). Also in that work, the Eastern Nilotes have been designated as the Plains Nilotes, and the Western Nilotes as the River-Lake Nilotes.
2. Other spellings of the name Dadog, which occur in the earlier literature, include Tatog, Tatoga, and Datog.

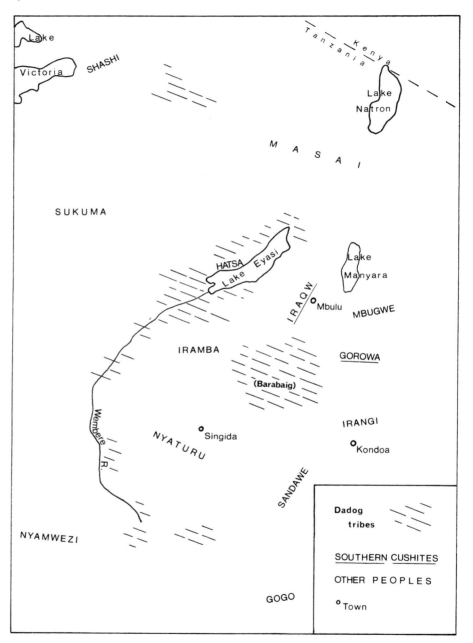

MAP 1.   Modern Distribution of the Dadog

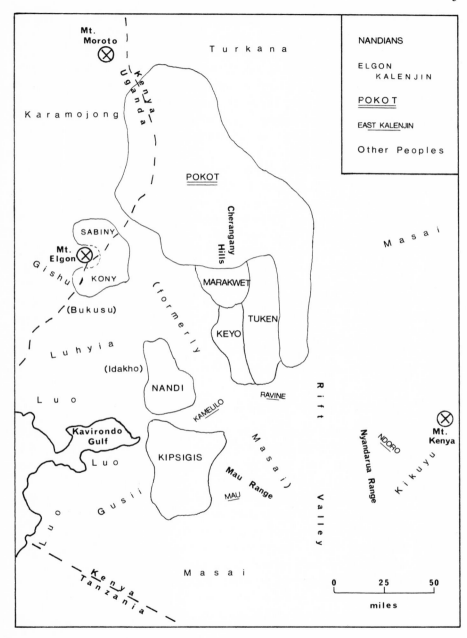

MAP 2. Modern Distribution of the Kalenjin

south along the Sibiti River from Lake Eyasi; and the Ghumbieg, Mangadg, Reimojig, Daragwajeg, and Bianjid, who extend along the Wembere River in Singida area as far south as Itigi. None of these subtribes numbers more than a few thousand. The Gisamjeng are in the process of being assimilated by the Southern Cushitic–speaking Iraqw pressing in from the north, while several others are gradually being absorbed by the Bantu peoples they live among. All the Dadog, including the Barabaig, live in areas suitable to cattle-raising and in the past have generally emphasized herding more than cultivation in their subsistence practices and value systems.

Kalenjin peoples include the Kony, Pok, Bongomek, Sabiny, Nandi, Kipsigis, Terik, Keyo, Tuken, Marakwet, Pokot, Akie, and various of the so-called Dorobo of the Kenya rift-valley country. The first four peoples live about Mount Elgon, the next six in the highlands south and southeast from Mount Elgon; the Pokot live to the north of these peoples. The Akie are hunting people who live among the Masai of south Masai area in Tanzania. Except for the Akie and the Kenya Dorobo, who were formerly all hunter-gatherers in economy, the Kalenjin peoples are herders and cultivators. All together the Kalenjin number about a million. The largest tribe, the Kipsigis, has 350,000 persons; the second largest, the Nandi, has from 150,000 to 200,000; and the Pokot, Tuken, and Keyo each number about 100,000. The Dorobo bands, at the other extreme, may have only a few hundred members apiece, while other Kalenjin groups range in size between the two extremes.

THE SOURCES FOR EARLY SOUTHERN NILOTIC HISTORY

Written sources provide information on the Southern Nilotic past covering no more than the last hundred years, while oral tradition nowhere carries the story back more than two or three centuries before that. Yet Southern Nilotic–speaking peoples have been living in East Africa for at least the last two millennia. Remembered history tells nothing of their participation in the momentous events of East African history in the first millennium A.D. and nothing of the still earlier developments which identified and shaped the ancestral Southern Nilotic community. The reconstruction of this history depends on linguistic, ethnographical, and archaeological evidence.

Of these sources for historical reconstruction, linguistics is least used and understood and yet in many ways is potentially the most fruitful. For instance, the vocabulary of any language is sufficient to handle the whole culture of the speakers of the languages. Thus in a good set of linguistic evidence of a people's existence will be the words which describe all aspects of their culture, whereas in a good set of archaeological evidence for the same people there will be only the relics of material aspects of their culture. Occasionally the archaeologist may be able to make some secondary inferences about nonmaterial culture, such as about the family structure from the layout of the home, but he can make such inferences with neither the degree of certainty nor the detail that the historian who uses linguistics can.

The value of archaeological evidence is that the culture it discovers can be located precisely by the distributions of the sites at which the culture has left the material evidence of its existence and can be dated in general terms on an absolute time scale by radiocarbon dating of its remains. When a people discovered by linguistic evidence can be identified in the archaeological record—through correlation of what linguistic data reveal about their material culture and their likely location and date with the results of archaeological investigation—then the better information linguistic evidence can give on the people and their culture in general will be supplemented by the better information archaeology can give on the location and date of the society.

Ethnographic evidence is, of course, necessary for understanding the present significance, and for reconstructing the past context, of culture words used as linguistic evidence for social history. But it is also useful as corroborating evidence for conclusions drawn on the basis of linguistic evidence, and it can often serve as basic evidence where linguistic evidence is insufficient to answer a question.

For this study the bulk of the evidence utilized is linguistic. The emphasis on linguistic evidence is an expression of the secondary purpose of this study of Southern Nilotic history: the demonstration of the usefulness of linguistic evidence in the reconstruction of African history. Ethnographical evidence is drawn on in many cases, however, to back up or add to a discussion. But the archaeology of East Africa is so very poorly known at this time that only a very limited use of archaeological data is feasible.

THE COLLECTION OF EVIDENCE

The collection of linguistic evidence was facilitated by the use of a standard cultural vocabulary of about 1200 entries, constructed specifically for this purpose. The entries were chosen on the basis of wide use and importance in the vocabularies of East African and, especially, Southern Nilotic cultures. The cultural vocabulary thus constructed provided maximum evidence for the investigation of earlier social and economic practices, while at the same time it consisted of those domains of vocabulary which experience has shown to be most subject to word-borrowing. On the one hand, it allowed the study of the social and economic development of the people speaking the language for which a cultural vocabulary was gathered, while on the other hand it allowed recognition of the impact of other peoples in this history insofar as that impact was revealed by the presence of loanwords in the collected vocabulary.

Tracing the threads of historical development that connect the histories of the Southern Nilotes with the histories of other East African peoples required the investigation of vocabularies of more than thirty East African dialects. To supplement the usually inadequate published materials on these dialects, the writer personally collected the standard culture-word vocabulary for approximately twenty languages and dialects.

Just as it was not feasible to collect full dictionaries of every language to be studied, so it was not feasible to collect the culture-word vocabulary for every possible dialect that might contain lexical evidence bearing on Southern Nilotic history. Dialects in several relevant languages are numerous, and, in any case, collecting a vocabulary of a dialect closely related to another will usually add very little evidence about early periods to that gained from collecting words for the first dialect. The problem of selection was resolved by choosing, out of any language or groups of closely related dialects, one or two dialects as representative of the group and, for this one or two, collecting the cultural vocabulary. For the Bantu-speaking Gishu and Luhyia peoples the Bukusu and Idakho dialects were chosen as representative; for the Bantu living along the southeast of Lake Victoria, the Jita dialect; and for the Masai, the pastoral Masai dialect as spoken in far southern Kenya. For the dialectally diverse Southern Nilotic Kalenjin, as principals in this story, a number of dialects had to be collected. Chosen were the Kony dialect, as representative of the Kalenjin speech of Mount Elgon; western Pokot; Akie; Nandi, as representative of the Nandian dialects; and Kamelilo Dorobo. For Dadog-speaking Southern Nilotes the Barabaig dialect was studied because it could be presumed to have been least affected by very recent loanwords from neighboring Bantu and Southern Cushitic languages, which might have replaced some earlier loanwords and thus to some extent obscured what could be learned from the study of its vocabulary. Short supplementary vocabulary collections were also made from the Kwaya dialect of the southeast Victoria shore, for the Arusha dialect of Masai, and for the Keyo, Tuken, and Marakwet dialects of the Kalenjin group. Where published sources for additional languages or dialects of any of the languages existed, they also were drawn on for evidence.

In addition to the culture-word list, a small collection of what might be called basic words—such as names for major parts of the body and verbs for universally recognized actions like "to go" and "to eat"—was made for most of the languages.[3] Word-borrowing is rare in such parts of the vocabulary, and so the presence or lack of loanwords there is a measure of the strength of the influence represented by the loanword set.

What must be understood is that the attempt here at a history of the early Southern Nilotes is not a final statement on the Southern Nilotic role in East African history. Rather it is a particular application of a methodology which historians must use if they are to convert the earlier eras of the African past into a rich and human history. For Southern Nilotic history it is only an outline of what can be said when finally the knowledge gained from ethnology, archaeology, and other disciplines can be integrated into it. But it is a necessary first step. Without it the right questions cannot be asked; insights once missed will be missed still.

3. For the purpose of this study a basic word is defined as one of the ninety words listed in Appendix A.1.

CHAPTER 2

Linguistic Sources for Southern Nilotic History

LANGUAGE RELATIONSHIP AS A FRAMEWORK FOR HISTORY

In reconstructing the history of eras for which there are neither documentary sources nor oral traditions, linguistic evidence holds much the same position that documentary evidence holds in the reconstruction of histories of literate periods. On it the basic structure of the history can be built, and evidence drawn from other sources can allow modification or elaboration of this structure. Taken together, the data drawn from the languages of the Southern Nilotes and of their modern neighbors can be used to set up a framework of Southern Nilotic history and to reconstruct many of the outside contacts of the Southern Nilotes and something of the patterns of cultural change and continuity among the Southern Nilotes during that history (see Map 3).

A chronological framework for Southern Nilotic history is inherent in the scheme of genetic relationships of the Southern Nilotic languages. On the deeper level of these relationships the Southern Nilotic languages constitute one branch among three which together form the Nilotic language group; the other branches are Eastern Nilotic and Western Nilotic.[1] Internally the Southern Nilotic languages divide into two subgroups, Dadog and Kalenjin. Kalenjin in turn separates into at least five coordinate[2] dialect groups. These relationships can be outlined as follows:[3]

Nilotic language group
1. Eastern Nilotic branch

1. The Eastern Nilotic branch consists of such languages as Bari, Lotuko, Teso, Karamojong, Masai, and Ongamo; the Western Nilotic branch, of Dinka and Nuer, Burun, and the Luo dialects. For the classification followed here see J. H. Greenberg, *The Languages of Africa* (Bloomington: Indiana University Research Center in Anthropology, Folklore, and Linguistics, 1963), and Oswin Köhler, *Geschichte der Erforschung der Nilotischen Sprachen* (Berlin: Reimer, 1955). On the position of Southern Nilotic see also Greenberg, "'Nilo-Hamitic' and Hamito-Semitic: A Reply," *Africa*, XXVII (1957). The writer has investigated the evidence and reaches similar conclusions.
2. That is, each is equally distant from each other one.
3. Only Southern Nilotic is subclassified here, because the topic is Southern Nilotic history (see Appendix A.7). But both Eastern and Western Nilotic can be divided into several subgroups.

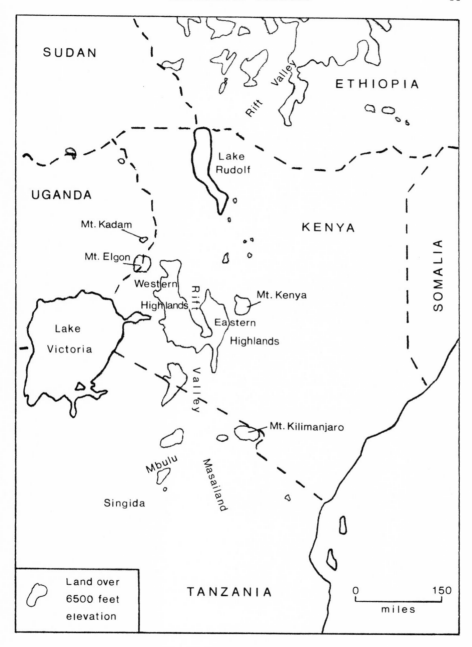

MAP 3.   The Countries of Southern Nilotic History

2. Western Nilotic branch
3. Southern Nilotic branch
   a) Dadog subgroup (Dadog dialects)
   b) Kalenjin subgroup[4]
        (1) Nandian (Nandi, Kipsigis, Keyo, Tuken, and Marakwet dialects)
        (2) Pokot
        (3) Elgon (Kony, Sabiny, Pok, and Bongomek dialects)
        (4) East Kalenjin[5] (various Kalenjin Dorobo dialects of Kenya)
        (5) South Kalenjin (Akie dialect)

Genetic relationship implies a common ancestor language, called a proto-language, from which the related languages descend. The more distant the relationship between the languages, the earlier in time the protolanguage was spoken. The Nandian dialects go back, thus, to a common ancestor, proto-Nandian; proto-Nandian, along with the other Kalenjin dialects, goes back to an earlier proto-Kalenjin speech; Dadog and Kalenjin together descend from a still earlier proto–Southern Nilotic language; and finally proto–Southern Nilotic was itself the descendant of proto-Nilotic, the ancestor language of all the modern Nilotic languages.

Each protolanguage requires the past existence of a community speaking that language. Thus a sequence of communities existing at various times in the past can be set up. The earliest community is that which spoke proto-Nilotic. Southern Nilotic history begins with the development of the earliest separate Southern Nilotic speech out of one of the dialects of proto-Nilotic. At a later date the proto–Southern Nilotic community, defined as the speakers of the immediate common ancestor language of Dadog and Kalenjin, existed. Still later, the proto-Kalenjin community came into being, and finally such communities as that which spoke proto-Nandian developed out of the proto-Kalenjin.

There are, then, in a linguistic framework of Southern Nilotic history, four major nodes, in order from most ancient to most recent: (1) the proto-Nilotic

---

4. Cf. Appendix A.1. This subclassification is new and is based on the writer's recent research. Previous classifications separated Kalenjin into two dialect groups, one consisting of Pokot and the other of all the rest of the Kalenjin dialects.

5. This is not claimed here to be more than a convenient label for the various dialects spoken by the Kalenjin hunter-gatherers who live in scattered bands about the rift-valley country of Kenya. It may define a valid genetic grouping of dialects; see Appendix A.6 for possible evidence. But there are far too few data on these dialects for this question to be answered yet.

period, (2) the proto–Southern Nilotic period; (3) the proto-Kalenjin period, and (4) the proto-Nandian period.[6]

The community at each nodal period would not necessarily have been a united people speaking a language without dialects. In fact, the more usual case would probably have been a cluster of several very closely associated peoples speaking closely related dialects of a single protolanguage. As with all languages, the protolanguage was continually undergoing change. As long as the people speaking the language lived together in a relatively small area, they would remain in easy communication with one another, and changes appearing in their speech would tend to be shared by all of them. The language would change but would remain one language. But as the language came to be spoken over a much larger area, communication between its speakers in widely separated places might well break down. Subsequently, changes appearing in the language might not affect the language everywhere but only as it was spoken in parts of its territory. Thus new dialect differences would appear and old ones would grow greater in different parts of the country. The continuing of this process would mark the breakup of the nodal community and of the proto-language spoken in it. Eventually the differences would grow so great that the former dialects of the protolanguage would become separate languages, no longer mutually intelligible. The breakup of the proto-Kalenjin community seems, for instance, to have developed according to this general pattern. A more abrupt breakup of a nodal community could follow upon the irruptive settlement of a new people which cut the old territory of the community in two or upon the sudden emigration of some of the speakers of the proto-language to a new and distant area.

CULTURES OF NODAL COMMUNITIES

Something can generally be said about the culture of each nodal community. The evidence derives from the linguists' reconstruction of vocabulary of the protolanguage spoken by the community. In the reconstructible vocabulary, of course, will appear words dealing with the work, thought, and other activities of the people who spoke the protolanguage. For the proto–Southern Nilotic vocabulary there can be reconstructed the words "iron" and "to forge" and many words dealing with livestock and herding; so it is clear that

---

6 Proto-Nandian was chosen as the most recent node because the Nandian dialects are the best-known Kalenjin dialects. The proto-Elgon period, of course, also fell between the end of the proto-Kalenjin era and the present and so also could have been a suitable node.

the proto–Southern Nilotes knew of iron-working and in addition were well acquainted with pastoral pursuits. If the relationships within a language family are very distant, the amount of reconstructible vocabulary is very small, and of course the amount of evidence bearing on the culture of the people who spoke the protolanguage of the family may be so small as to be of no use. Southern Nilotic history is generally recent enough for a good deal to be said about earlier Southern Nilotic cultures.

The usual criteria for reconstructing a word of the vocabulary of a proto-language are that modern forms of the word, called "reflexes," occur in dialects belonging to at least two of the coordinate subgroups into which the descendant languages of that protolanguage can be classified and that the modern shapes of the words in the different dialects be relatable according to a system of regular sound correspondences.[7] To be reconstructible for the proto–Southern Nilotic language, a word would have to be found today in Dadog and at least one Kalenjin dialect; then the differences between the shape it took in Dadog and its shape in Kalenjin would have to be different in a predictable manner. Dadog *ge:š-*,[8] "leg," can be said to show regular correspondence with Akie (Kalenjin) *ke:l-*, with the same meaning, because words that have *g* in Dadog have *k* in Akie, *e:* where Akie has *e:*, and *š* for many Akie *l*.

On this basis Dadog and Akie words for "leg" are termed cognates, and a form *ke:lʸ-* is reconstructed as the proto–Southern Nilotic word for "leg." The middle phoneme is pronounced the same in both Dadog and Akie, *e:*, so there is no reason to think that the proto–Southern Nilotic pronunciation was radically different. The *k, however, was arbitrarily chosen to represent the original proto–Southern Nilotic phoneme which became *g* in Dadog and *k* in Akie and other Kalenjin dialects. Evidence is lacking to determine whether *k* derives from original *g* or *g* from the very similarly articulated *k*. As for the final phoneme of the word, *l* is a quite different sound from *š*, and neither is directly derivable from the other. In this instance it seems best to postulate an original Southern Nilotic phoneme intermediate in articulation to *l* and *š* and

7. The reader should be warned that the following discussion constitutes only the barest introduction to the problems of word reconstruction. For a fuller handling of the principles and methods of reconstruction he should read Henry M. Hoenigswald, *Language Change and Linguistic Reconstruction* (Chicago: University of Chicago Press, 1960), and other technical works.

8. A list of linguistic signs used in this book and their approximate pronunciations will be found on pp. 90–91.

out of which both *l* and *š* could have developed. A palatal lateral *lʸ* fits this requirement; it is articulated with a similar tongue motion as an *l* but in the same part of the mouth as an *š*.[9]

To be considered cognates, words in different languages must, of course, have some kind of correspondence in meaning as well as systematic correspondence in sounds. In the example cited, the meaning is the same for both Dadog and Kalenjin forms and so presumably was the same in the proto–Southern Nilotic form. But cognate words can have quite different meanings in their modern versions. The Dadog reflex of proto–Southern Nilotic **so:m-* has the meaning "slave," while the Kalenjin forms of the root have the meaning "uncircumcised girl." But these differences in meaning can quite easily be reconciled. Circumcision was the event which certified that a person had become a fully adult member of Southern Nilotic society. A slave was like an uncircumcised person in lacking status in the society. The proto–Southern Nilotic meaning of the word would presumably have been "uncircumcised person"; in Kalenjin the meaning became narrowed to "uncircumcised girl," while in Dadog the meaning was first extended metaphorically to include all persons without adult status, then narrowed to mean slaves only.

A much less certain proto–Southern Nilotic word is one the shape of which would be reconstructed as **a:ra:k-*. The apparent Dadog reflex signifies a wooden tray or low bowl; the proposed Nandi (Kalenjin) reflex means "empty sword sheath." What both meanings have in common is the idea of an open or empty container, but otherwise there is little resemblance between a broad wooden container and a long thin leather one. Very possibly the two words are cognates. But the probability of this conclusion is far lower than the near certainty which attaches to the reconstruction of a word like proto–Southern Nilotic **so:m-*. Most conclusions here about Southern Nilotic history which are based on vocabulary reconstructions are based on reconstructions with probabilities of at least as high an order as that of **so:m-*. If a conclusion has a lesser probability, it is modified by adverbial expressions such as "possibly" or "very possibly."

Sometimes a word can be reconstructed for the protolanguage of a language group even though today it occurs in only one of the coordinate branches of the group. The requirement for reconstruction is that the word already had been

9. This reconstruction is in fact confirmed by comparative evidence from the more distantly related Eastern and Western Nilotic languages.

used in a language ancestral to the protolanguage itself. Words for "beehive" built on a stem *moi:ŋ(k)- are found only in Kalenjin, but the word must nevertheless be reconstructed for proto–Southern Nilotic because it already existed in the late pre–Southern Nilotic dialect from which proto–Southern Nilotic itself derived. The original form of the word, *mori:ŋ(k)-, has lost an r, a Southern Nilotic sound change which operated only at the end of pre–Southern Nilotic times; to show the sound change, the word had to have been in use by Southern Nilotes at least that early. A different kind of example is Dadog æ:no:g, "milk." This word must have been used in proto–Southern Nilotic because it belongs to a set of loanwords from Eastern Cushitic borrowed by the ancestors of the proto–Southern Nilotes earlier during the pre–Southern Nilotic period.

LOCATING NODAL COMMUNITIES

It is usually possible also, in very general terms at least, to suggest the region in which the people speaking a protolanguage lived. This sort of inference follows from consideration of the present geographical distribution of subgroups of languages descended from the particular protolanguage whose ancient home area is being sought. A very good example is provided by proto-Kalenjin, for which a close determination of the original territory can be made. One modern Kalenjin subgroup, South Kalenjin, is represented by a dialect spoken in southern Masailand in Tanzania, but all the rest of the subgroups of Kalenjin dialects are tightly clustered, centering in the western highlands of Kenya from Mount Elgon in the northwest to the rift valley in the southeast (see Map 2). The Kalenjin homeland is probably to be located, then, in the western highlands because, if the Kalenjin dialects had developed elsewhere, it is highly unlikely that all but one of them, despite separate histories, would have ended up clustered in the same general region.

Conversely, the technique allows only the most general indications about the country of the proto–Southern Nilotic community. The languages of the two Southern Nilotic subgroups are spoken today in widely separated areas—Dadog in north central Tanzania and the Kalenjin dialects in southwestern Kenya—and each group might just as well have been brought from the territory now inhabited by the other, or both might just as likely have come from a third area where neither is spoken today. All that can be said is that each is spoken in country near the eastern rift valley of East Africa and east of

Lake Victoria and that therefore the land of their common ancestor was most probably somewhere in that rather vast region running from northern Kenya to central Tanzania. The location of the proto–Southern Nilotic community simply cannot be pinned down any more closely without using other evidence.[10]

LOANWORDS AS EVIDENCE OF CONTACT BETWEEN PEOPLES

While the internal history of the Southern Nilotes can be approached through the study of Southern Nilotic language relationships and linguistic history, the context of Southern Nilotic developments can be studied through the evidence of Southern Nilotic loanwords in the languages of other East African peoples and of loanwords from other languages in Southern Nilotic speech. In preliterate times the presence of a loanword in a language meant, at the least, contact of some speakers of the language with some speakers of the language from which the word came. A whole set of loanwords from one language in another would require extensive interaction between the speakers of the two languages and widespread bilingualism in the languages. The crucial point is that the interaction would require that the two peoples speaking the two languages be neighbors or near neighbors at the period of word-borrowing.[11]

In interpreting the contacts indicated by word-borrowing, the necessary first step is to determine the sources of individual loanwords. There are several methods of loanword determination, and it should be noted that the different methods give conclusions of differing degrees of probability. Occasionally a single loanword determination may have so high a probability of being correct that tentative historical conclusions can be based on it. But in general it is the accumulation of loanword evidence that proves a case. While a particular proposed loanword in a language may have entered the language other than by direct borrowing from the proposed source language, it would be very unlikely that a whole set of probable loanwords should all have entered the language by other means.

10. The classic monograph on the techniques of inferring place of origin of peoples or traits from their modern distribution is Edward Sapir, *Time Perspective in Aboriginal American Culture* (Ottawa: Government Printing Bureau, 1916). It is essential reading for the student of predocumentary history.
11. Long-distance trade by caravans or itinerant traders can be disregarded as a factor in loanword spread because such enterprise is unlikely for the peoples and periods studied. Local trade between neighbors, on the other hand, was probably an important form of early contact.

The strongest criteria for loanword determination tend to be morphological and phonological. By these criteria the presence and source of a loanword are indicated by the occurrence of features in the word which cannot be explained by grammatical or sound changes in the language in which the word occurs but which can be explained in terms of such developments in another language. An example of the application of criteria of morphology in determining the source of a loanword is provided by Bukusu *eaiyua*, "ax."[12] In the Kalenjin dialects the same word occurs as *aiyua*. The final *-ua* is a very common suffix, that is, a morphological feature, of Kalenjin nouns, but it is not a Bukusu noun suffix. Thus the source of the word in Bukusu must be considered to have been a Kalenjin-related dialect. This sort of determination is usually of a very high order of probability.

It is also possible to make use of negative morphological criteria in loanword determination. Bukusu *luteeka*, "bamboo," provides an example.[13] Several Kalenjin dialects call bamboo *te:ka*; their form of the word lacks the Bukusu prefix *lu-*. Since the prefix is a necessary part of the word in Bukusu, the Kalenjin dialects would have maintained the prefix in their form of the word if they had borrowed it from Bukusu. As the word is found with this particular shape only in Kalenjin and Bukusu and is not a loanword from Bukusu, then the Bukusu word is in all likelihood borrowed from a Kalenjin-related dialect. But the probability of this conclusion is not so great as that of the determination of the loanword "ax," because the possibility that both the Bukusu and the Kalenjin dialects borrowed the word from a third, now lost, source language cannot be entirely ruled out.

Sometimes a word is old enough in a source language that the morphological rules according to which it was originally derived can no longer be worked out, or its derivation is ambiguous in that the word could conceivably be derived according to rules of word formation in the borrowing language as well as in the source language. In some such cases it is nevertheless possible to apply a kind of criterion of derivation to determine the loanword source. This criterion can be applied when in one language a whole series of words built on a common stem occurs, while, in a second language, only one of the words built on that stem can be found. Kalenjin dialects, for example, have a series of words for aspects of the practice of magic built on a stem *sa:k-/*se:k-*, no longer existing as an independent word. These

12. See also Appendix D.11.
13. See Appendix D.11.

secondary words include Nandi *kipsakeiyuo*, "magician," and Kony *sekut*, "to bewitch (cattle)." In Masai the verb "to bewitch" appears as *-sakut*, apparently from the same secondary word as Kony *sekut*.[14] Since the word is one of a series of derivative words in Kalenjin but is isolated in Masai, it must be considered original in Kalenjin but borrowed by Masai.

A variety of phonological criteria can be used in loanword determination. As an example, Iraqw *mayšot*, "sack," must be a borrowing of Dadog *mišo:d* because it shows a sound change which can be explained only in terms of Dadog sound history. The original proto–Southern Nilotic version of the word contained the phoneme l^y, which became *š* only in Dadog. A different kind of phonological criterion is exemplified by the determination that proto-Kalenjin **mak-*, "hippopotamus," was a borrowing of Southern Cushitic (proto–West Rift) **max-*, with the same meaning.[15] The Southern Cushites cannot have borrowed their word from the Kalenjin because their languages, having both *x* and *k* phonemes, would have taken the word over from Kalenjin unchanged; but the Kalenjin dialects, lacking the *x* phoneme, would have had to replace Southern Cushitic *x* with their own nearest equivalent phoneme, *k*, as indeed appears to be the case. A third phonological criterion of a loanword is the appearance in the word of a foreign sound borrowed along with the foreign word. Pokot *adir*, "oryx," is shown to be a borrowing of Karamojong-Teso *adir* by its maintenance of implosive *d*, a sound foreign to earlier Kalenjin dialects but original in the Karamojong-Teso dialects.[16] Phonological criteria can allow near certainty of determination; Iraqw *mayšot* is an example of such a determination. The second, and sometimes the third, type of phonological criterion provides conclusions of lower probability. It is not entirely impossible, for instance, that both Kalenjin and Southern Cushitic languages borrowed their words for "hippopotamus" from some extinct third language or that the Kalenjin borrowed the word from another language which in turn had earlier borrowed it from a Southern Cushitic language.

Distributional criteria can also be used to indicate the direction of word-borrowing. These criteria apply if it can be demonstrated that a word is older in languages of one language family than in languages of another family. For example, the verb *-nab-*, "to sew," is used in many Luhyia and

14. See Appendix F.3.
15. See Appendix B.3.
16. See Appendix G.1

Gishu (Bantu) dialects; but all these dialects are mutually intelligible or very nearly mutually intelligible, so that the word need not have been in Luhyia-Gishu more than several centuries. In the Southern Nilotic language group, on the other hand, the related verb *na:p was already in the proto–Southern Nilotic vocabulary 1500 to 2000 years ago.[17] It is thus an older word in the Southern Nilotic languages than in Bantu and is to be considered a loanword in the Luhyia and Gishu dialects, presumably from a Southern Nilotic source.[18]

INTERPRETING LOANWORD EVIDENCE

To be useful as historical evidence, loanwords in a language have, of course, to be grouped by relative times of borrowing as well as by source. One method is to date the appearance of a word by its occurrence in a protolanguage. If the word can be reconstructed for a particular protolanguage, then it was borrowed at least as early as the period when that protolanguage was still spoken. If the loanword belongs to a whole set of loanwords borrowed in the same general era from a particular source language, it is often possible also to put an earlier limit on the borrowing of the word and the set of words it belongs to. If, as an example, the set of words occurs in language A but not in related language B, then the words must have been borrowed after A and B became separate, that is, after the breakup of the protolanguage which was the common ancestor of A and B. A set of loanwords from a particular source language which can be reconstructed as occurring in proto-Kalenjin but which does not appear in Dadog and therefore cannot be reconstructed for earlier proto–Southern Nilotic would be presumed to have been borrowed between the end of the proto–Southern Nilotic period and the end of the proto-Kalenjin period.

A difficulty with this method appears when one language descending from a particular protolanguage continued to borrow words from the same source language as had the earlier protolanguage. This loan stratum in the descendant

17. See Appendix D.9.
18. What cannot be excluded completely, of course, is the possibility once again that both language groups could have got their words for "to sew" from some third source or that the Luhyia-Gishu word could have been borrowed from some other language which had itself borrowed the word from Southern Nilotic. For further discussion of the problems of loanword determination see E. J. A. Henderson, "The Phonology of Loanwords in Some Southeast Asian Languages," *Transactions of the Philological Society*, 1951; and, for African languages in particular, see J. H. Greenberg, "Linguistic Evidence for the Influence of the Kanuri on the Hausa," *Journal of African History*, I (1960), 205–12.

language will consist of words which appear only in the vocabulary of that language. But in any descendant language some of the words originally borrowed by the protolanguage will after a time drop out of use as part of the normal process of change in a language. Each descendant will eventually come to have a few words borrowed in the protolanguage period but now retained only by the one descendant language and lost in the others. Occurring now only in the particular descendant language, these few words will not be individually distinguishable from words borrowed from the same source by the descendant language in later times.

To show that some of the loanwords limited to the descendant language indeed indicate a loanword period peculiar to the language and that they are not all simply left over from the protolanguage period requires that the particular descendant have strikingly more loanwords from the source language than the other descendants of the same protolanguage. For instance, if twenty loanwords from a source language could be reconstructed for a proto-ABC language while, let us say, four words from the same source occurred only in descendant language A, five only in descendant language B, and two only in descendant language C, there would be insufficient reason to think any of the descendants of the proto-ABC people had special later contacts with speakers of the source language of the loanwords. The loanwords peculiar to A, B, or C would not necessarily be other than words borrowed by proto-ABC which happened to have been retained only in one or another of its descendants. But if C had fifteen loanwords peculiar to it, for example, while A and B still had four and five, respectively, then C's excess of loanwords from the source language would require special explanation, namely, that the people speaking C had contacts with the source-language people in which the A and B peoples did not share.

A better dating of loanwords can often be obtained by study of sound changes in the borrowing and source languages. The basic criterion of this method is that if a sound change that has operated generally in a language has operated in a particular word in the language, then that word was used in the language at the period of the sound change. This criterion can be used to show the proper age of a loanword when the first method gives inadequate evidence. For example, a Bantu loanword *moi:ŋ(k)-*,[19] "beehive," occurs today only in Kalenjin of the two Southern Nilotic subgroups. On this

19. This is the proto-Kalenjin form reconstructed by the writer. The proto–Southern Nilotic form would have had the same reconstruction.

evidence alone it could only be said that the word had to have been borrowed before the close of the proto-Kalenjin period. But in fact the word was borrowed much earlier, even before the proto–Southern Nilotic period: from its original Southern Nilotic form *mori:ŋ(k)-* the *r* has been lost, a sound change that occurred at the beginning of the proto–Southern Nilotic period.

The method can also be used to narrow down the possible period during which a word could have been borrowed. In a set of words borrowed during a long period determined by the first method, an individual word of the set could be shown to have been borrowed early or late in the interval depending on whether or not it evidenced a sound change that had operated in the donor or recipient language during the period. In the time since the breakup of the common ancestor of Iraqw and Burungi, Dadog has borrowed numerous words from Iraqw, at least some of these words quite early in the period. Dadog *sirbi:d*, "waterpot," has *b* where modern Iraqw has *w*, for instance; and since early Iraqwan *b* had already become *w* even before the Gorowa separated from the Iraqw, the Dadog word had to have been borrowed before that time. Iraqw and Gorowa, though interintelligible, are now quite distinct dialects, and so the first Dadog contact with Iraqwan peoples had to have begun at least several centuries ago. The value of this method of sound changes is that it can date individual word-borrowings, whereas the method of occurrence in a protolanguage can be used only with sets of loanwords.

HISTORICAL IMPLICATIONS OF LOANWORDS

The interpretation of the histories behind various intensities and types of word-borrowing must rely on evidence which often is ambiguous in the present state of knowledge about languages in contact. But some indication of the possible histories that can underlie different types of loanword activity can be obtained from test cases of East African peoples whose histories during recent loanword periods are known from oral tradition and documentary sources. It seems useful for the purposes of this study to distinguish four categories of loanword activity in East Africa.

1. *Intensive word-borrowing.* This category is defined by the presence of several basic words[20] among the loanwords of a particular loanword stratum in a language. The borrowing of a number of basic words is always accompanied in East African examples by heavy word-borrowing generally throughout

20. For discussion of the terms "basic" and "cultural vocabulary" see Chapter 1.

the cultural vocabulary. Over time the cultural words have a much higher attrition than basic words, and so after two or three millennia an intensive word-borrowing period may still be represented by several basic words but by only a few remaining culture words. The occurrence of several basic words among the loans is sufficient to indicate that the culture-word-borrowings must once have been many more and that one is therefore dealing with an early intensive word-borrowing period. The dialects of the Kalenjin-speaking Dorobo in Kenya provide recent examples of this type of borrowing. Kamelilo, for instance, has more than half a dozen Masai loanwords in the basic vocabulary, an extraordinary number, and numerous Masai loans among culture words. Other Kalenjin Dorobo dialects have been similarly affected by Masai contacts.[21] The word-borrowing activity in Dorobo stems from the fact that each small group has been isolated for the past several centuries within territory occupied by much more numerous, as well as economically and politically dominant, Masai-speaking people.

2. *Heavy general word-borrowing.* This category is defined by the general occurrence of numerous loanwords from a particular source language throughout the cultural vocabulary. Over time the number of discoverable loanwords from the period will become fewer. After one or two thousand years the former heavy general occurrence of the loanwords will be whittled down to a rather scattered occurrence of remaining loanwords through the cultural vocabulary. A recent example of heavy general word-borrowing is provided by Kenya Luo, which has borrowed a great number of words from a Bantu dialect closely related to the modern Luhyia dialects.[22] The loanwords have entered Luo as a result of the Luo expansion into the Kavirondo Gulf area in the past four centuries[23] and their assimilation of the Bantu peoples who preceded them. This sort of word-borrowing might also result from the type of influence exerted by the Masai on the Dorobo, only on a lesser scale or less long sustained. Masai loanwords in Akie, the language of the Kalenjin Dorobo of south Masailand, appear to constitute an example.

3. *Light general word-borrowing.* This category is defined by the occurrence of loanwords from a particular source in many parts of the cultural vocabulary

21. See Appendix G.2.
22. See Appendix H.4.
23. B. A. Ogot, *History of the Southern Luo* (Nairobi: East African Publishing House, 1967), I, 152.

though nowhere in large numbers. An example of this category are the scattered Luo loanwords in Gusii. The Gusii have for the past two centuries been in continual contact, if not conflict, with the neighboring and expanding Luo.[24] This type of borrowing might also result from a history similar to that described for the Luo in category 2 but where the previous language had much less impact on the language of the immigrants than Luhyia appears to have had on Luo. However, no recent East African language shifts which exemplify such a situation are known.

4. *Specific cultural word-borrowing*. This category includes the borrowing of a set of words restricted in reference to one area of culture and the borrowing of a single word for a single culture item. Such borrowing can be taken to indicate that the people speaking the source language of the loanwords were viewed as dominant in the specific cultural area of the loans or, when a single word is borrowed, that the people speaking the source language were probably the source of the item or trait indicated by the word. Swahili and English loanwords in East African languages generally exemplify these kinds of contacts.

This tentative categorization can, in conjunction with other data, be used to elucidate the testimony of many of the loanword sets relevant to the study of Southern Nilotic history. A Rift Southern Cushitic loanword set in proto-Kalenjin, for example, fits the category of heavy general word-borrowing. The borrowed words occur widely through the proto-Kalenjin cultural vocabulary and include even one basic word;[25] and even though a millennium or more has passed since the time of borrowing and the Rift language from which the words were borrowed was much different from any modern Southern Cushitic language, quite a number of such loanwords still can be discovered. The particular Rift Southern Cushites no longer exist and so presumably have been assimilated into later populations inhabiting their country. Thus the historical parallel with Luo and Bantu interaction in the Kavirondo region seems very close. Even as the Luo borrowed many words from the Bantu peoples they assimilated, so the ancestors of the Kalenjin incorporated their Rift-speaking predecessors while adopting many of their words.

24. *Ibid.*, Chapters 5, 6.
25. See Appendix B.3 and Chapter 6.

The historical significance of loanword sets is not always so easily determined. Categorization of kinds of loanword activity is as yet a rough tool, as is evident in the discussions of the various suggested categories. Still it is a useful supplement to the methods of discovering and interpreting the Southern Nilotic past through linguistic evidence.

CHAPTER 3

The Dating of Southern Nilotic History

CHRONOLOGICAL ASSUMPTIONS

The linguistic framework for Southern Nilotic history is a relative chronology of that history. The problem in dating Southern Nilotic history is to give some sort of absolute dates to events whose place in the relative time scale is known. The best evidence for dating will come from the eventual correlation of situations and developments required by the linguistic evidence with the cultures and material developments discovered by the methods of archaeology, because the archaeologist can give absolute dates of a sort to his discoveries. For now, the archaeology of East Africa is too little known to allow more than a few such correlations to be established. The chronology to be followed here for Southern Nilotic history will rely largely, then, on reasoning back from datable events of recent centuries.

A number of assumptions about population movement and language change and the time requirement of movement and change underlie the chronological interpretations given here to events of Southern Nilotic history. Not all these assumptions are immediately relevant to the initial discussion of the dating of Southern Nilotic communities, but as related suppositions they can best be considered together.

At the base of the assumptions lies the view that migration has rarely been a prodigious event in Africa, earth-shaking when it occurred. Instead, migration is a rather ordinary event in human affairs. People move because of war, famine, dissatisfaction with their status, scarcity of land, disease, natural catastrophe, and numerous other, personal reasons. They normally move only a short distance, perhaps only from one valley or one ridge to the next, and they move in relatively small groups. The Ngoni movements of the nineteenth century are notable simply because they were such exceptions to the usual pattern. Nearly always in Africa, migration involves the immigrants' assimilation of or into the previous population rather than the extermination or expulsion of the earlier people, and the population movement that does cause the indigenous people to adopt the immigrants' language is very often the cumulation of many small migrations.

26

Even at its most rapid, the complete shift of any local population from one language to another would not normally take less than about three generations, and it usually would require more time than that. Even if all the younger children in the community began at the same time no longer to learn the old language, still three generations would pass before those slightly older, who had learned the old language, would nearly all have died. And since such an immediate and complete shift to a new language would not usually occur, the process could be expected normally to take quite a bit longer than three generations.

The borrowing of a set of loanwords is also no short two- or ten-year affair. Most sets of loanwords probably represent several generations of contact between peoples speaking the donor and receptor languages of the word set. If we assume that the new language is first spoken fluently by children, a generation or so needs to be allowed for bilingualism to become sufficiently widespread among adult speakers of the receptor language for word-borrowing to become common. A further period of contact is then needed for the loan-words to become well established in the vocabulary of the receptor language. Most instances of really intensive word-borrowing probably represent the cumulative effect of many generations of interaction between speakers of donor and receptor languages.

While these assumptions inform the interpretation of many particular developments in Southern Nilotic history, the general chronological framework of that history rests in part on an assumption that cognate-counting in a basic vocabulary can indicate in a very general way the relative distances between languages that are fairly closely related. The distance of relationship between Kalenjin and Dadog is considered here as falling within the meaning of "fairly closely related." How this assumption is applied will become evident in the discussion of Southern Nilotic chronology.

A CHRONOLOGY FOR SOUTHERN NILOTIC HISTORY

The proto-Kalenjin period can be given a date by first locating the proto-Nandian period and then deriving its time separation from the proto-Kalenjin period by determining its relative linguistic distance from proto-Kalenjin speech. The Nandi-Keyo dialect split must date back at least to the 1600's if not earlier, because the Wuasinkishu Masai were already in the intervening country between Keyo and Nandi in the 1700's. In addition, the Keyo maintain an eight-set age cycle, whereas the Nandi had already lost one of those sets in the 1700's.[1] Moreover, oral tradition indicates that Nandi development as a separate people began in the 1600's, perhaps even early in the century.[2] But among Nandian dialects the difference between Tuken and Nandi and Marakwet and Nandi is if anything greater than the difference between Nandi and Keyo. Thus the earliest breakup of the Nandian dialects may go back even earlier, to the sixteenth or even fifteenth century; the proto-Nandian period should be dated probably not later than mid-millennium. Then by cognate-counting in a basic word list, the more distant Kalenjin dialects, such as Kony and Akie, turn out to be more than twice as distant from any of the Nandian dialects as the most divergent Nandian dialects are from one another. For example, Nandi and Tuken share 89 per cent of the words in a given basic vocabulary, while Nandi and Akie and Tuken and Akie share 77 and 74 per cent, respectively.[3] If, as has been suggested, the proto-Nandian community was in existence four or five hundred years ago, then the proto-Kalenjin period should be set approximately twice as long ago, somewhere in the range of eight to ten centuries before the present.[4]

By reference to this suggested date range for the proto-Kalenjin community, the proto–Southern Nilotes can in turn be given a very general date through cognate-counting. Dadog shares between 45 and 50 per cent of the basic vocabulary with each Kalenjin dialect, whereas the more distant Kalenjin dialects share around 75 per cent of the words in the same vocabulary.[5] Dadog thus appears more than twice as distant from any Kalenjin dialect as any Kalenjin dialects are from one another.[6] If the proto-Kalenjin period lies in the range of eight to ten centuries ago, the proto–Southern Nilotic period must be placed in the range of at least fifteen hundred to two thousand years ago.

1. G. W. B. Huntingford, *The Nandi of Kenya* (London: Routledge & Kegan Paul, 1953), p. 74.

2. *Ibid.*, p. 2.

3. See Appendix A.1.

4. The reasoning behind this statement is the following: If two Kalenjin dialects shared x per cent of words in a basic vocabulary after a time T, then, assuming a roughly similar rate of word loss, after an additional identical period T only roughly x per cent of the original x per cent would still be shared, or x^2 (x squared) per cent. After twice the time Nandi and Tuken would share 89 per cent squared, or 79 per cent of the basic vocabulary items, slightly higher than the percentages the Nandian dialects share with Akie. So twice as long a time is roughly assumed to separate Akie from Nandi or Tuken as is assumed to separate Nandi from Tuken.

5. See Appendix A.1.

6. See note 4 for explanation of this statement.

On the other hand, the correlation of linguistic and archaeological evidence requires that the ancestral Southern Nilotic community must not have broken up earlier than about two thousand years ago—earlier, that is, than the beginning of the Iron Age in East Africa.[7] The words for "iron" and for "forging" can be reconstructed for the proto–Southern Nilotic language:[8] the proto–Southern Nilotes were already an ironworking people. Thus the proto–Southern Nilotic community was probably in existence sometime in the first centuries of the Christian era.

The proto–Southern Nilotic period was preceded by the long pre–Southern Nilotic period, a span of perhaps two or three thousand years running from the time of the breakup of the proto-Nilotic community down to the beginning of proto–Southern Nilotic times. Cognate-counting suggests a length for the period somewhere in this range; the Eastern and Western Nilotic languages appear somewhat more than twice as distant from the Southern Nilotic languages as Dadog and Kalenjin dialects are from each other.[9] With such a great time depth, one may wish to avoid relying on cognate-counting as a tool for dating. What is clear, nevertheless, from the small amount of cognate-sharing between languages of different branches of Nilotic is that the time depth in Nilotic as a whole is very much greater than in the Southern Nilotic branch. The proto-Nilotic period may well have been as early as the third millennium B.C.; and the pre–Southern Nilotic period which followed it, the long period of the development of the proto–Southern Nilotic language out of a dialect of proto-Nilotic, may well have lasted two to three thousand years.

The crucial event considered here as marking the end of the pre–Southern Nilotic period and the beginning of the proto–Southern Nilotic era was a sound change, the loss of r before i in word-final syllables in the particular pre–Southern Nilotic dialect or set of dialects from which all the existing Southern Nilotic languages derive. The dialect or dialects in which r was thus lost constituted the proto–Southern Nilotic language. Pre–Southern Nilotic *mɔːri, "calf," became, for example, in proto–Southern Nilotic *mɔːi. This

7. Earliest Iron Age dates so far obtained in East Africa are slightly more recent than two thousand years ago. See Brian M. Fagan, "Radiocarbon Dates for Sub-Saharan Africa: V," *Journal of African History*, VIII (1967), 513–27.

8. See Appendix A.3.

9. Languages of different branches of Nilotic usually share about 15–20 per cent of words in the basic vocabulary used here for Southern Nilotic cognate counts, whereas Dadog and Kalenjin dialects share 45 and 50 per cent. Luo and Nandi share 20 per cent, for instance, while Masai and Nandi share 21 per cent and Masai and Luo 18 per cent.

event fell within the early years of the East African Iron Age, a conclusion directed by the lack of *r* in proto–Southern Nilotic **mece:i*, "branding iron." An *r* is attested in related words in other East African languages, for instance in Masai **mɪšɪr*, "to brand," and Ma'a *mišire*, "branding irons." Since loss of *r* in that position is a specifically Southern Nilotic development, it is necessary to reconstruct a pre–Southern Nilotic form with the *r* retained, thus: **mece:ri*. The very late pre–Southern Nilotes, at least, had branding irons and therefore apparently knew of iron. The sound change affected only some of the Southern Nilotic dialects spoken in East Africa at the end of pre–Southern Nilotic times; other pre–Southern Nilotic dialects which did not lose *r* before *i* in final syllables continued to be spoken in parts of East Africa down to much more recent periods.[10]

Southern Nilotic history begins thus with the breakup of the proto-Nilotic community perhaps as much as four or five thousand years ago; it continues through the pre–Southern Nilotic period, which ends finally about the beginning of the Iron Age in East Africa; the pre–Southern Nilotic period is followed in early centuries of the Christian era by the proto–Southern Nilotic period; the later proto-Kalenjin period is to be placed probably about the beginning centuries of the present millennium; and finally, the proto-Nandian period falls in the middle centuries of the current millennium. This dating of Southern Nilotic history can be summarized by a time line, as shown in Figure 1.

10. See Chapter 5. The possibility cannot be entirely ruled out that the word originally referred to a "branding stone" but later, when iron became known, was everywhere adapted to refer to the iron instrument. But in any case Bantu peoples were already settling in East Africa by the end of pre–Southern Nilotic times (Appendix E.1) and, by the time of their settlement there, can be presumed to have known of iron.

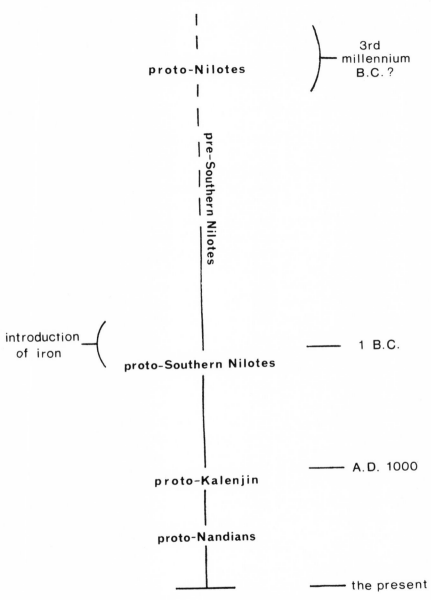

FIGURE 1.   Time Line of Southern Nilotic History

CHAPTER 4

The Origins of Southern Nilotic Society

THE PRE–SOUTHERN NILOTIC PERIOD

The origins of Southern Nilotic culture lie in the long pre–Southern Nilotic period. The culture of the proto–Southern Nilotes was no simple derivation from the culture of their linguistic ancestors, the proto-Nilotes. In particular, of overwhelming impact on pre–Southern Nilotic development were Southern Nilotic contacts with Eastern Cushites.[1] Then, toward the close of the pre–Southern Nilotic period, the Southern Nilotes came under Southern Cushitic influence and also had contacts with early Bantu peoples.

On the basis of the sequence of these contacts of the Southern Nilotes with other peoples, the pre–Southern Nilotic period can be divided into three parts: (1) the early pre–Southern Nilotic era, extending from the end of the proto-Nilotic period to the beginning of Eastern Cushitic domination of the Southern Nilotes; (2) the middle pre–Southern Nilotic era, the time of Eastern Cushitic dominance in Southern Nilotic history; and (3) the late pre–Southern Nilotic era, the period of the settlement of the Southern Nilotic peoples in southern Kenya and adjoining far northern Tanzania and of the beginning of Southern Nilotic interaction with the Southern Cushites and Bantu of those regions.

The late pre–Southern Nilotic period came to an end, of course, near the beginning of the East African Iron Age. It need not have begun but a few centuries before, perhaps in the second half of the last millennium B.C. On the other hand, Southern Nilotic settlement in East Africa could just possibly have begun as early as the beginning of that millennium: the removal of the lower incisors, an ancient Nilotic trait, was practiced by the inhabitants of the Njoro River Cave site, which has been given a radiocarbon date of about 1000 B.C.[2]

1. Modern Eastern Cushites are the Galla, Somali, Afar, Saho, Rendille, Baiso, Konso, Geleba, Kambatta, Gudella, and a number of other peoples of the far southeast of the Ethiopian highlands.
2. Sonia Cole, *The Prehistory of East Africa* (London: George Weidenfeld & Nicolson, 1963), pp. 286–93, and Brian M. Fagan, "Radiocarbon Dates for Sub-Saharan Africa—I," *Journal of African History*, II (1961).

The placing of the Eastern Cushitic contact period in a middle pre–Southern Nilotic era preceding the Southern Cushitic contacts of the late pre–Southern Nilotes is on geographical rather than linguistic grounds. Linguistic evidence places the Eastern Cushitic loanword set in Southern Nilotic before the loss-of-*r* sound change, that is, sometime generally in pre–Southern Nilotic times.[3] But otherwise pre–Southern Nilotic sound history is too little known to allow other such evidence to be brought to bear. The geographical consideration is that the most likely area of contact between the pre–Southern Nilotes and the Eastern Cushites was in the far north of East Africa or on the Ethiopian highland fringes, near the original homeland of the Eastern Cushites[4] and near where most of the Eastern Cushitic peoples are still found today. So far there is no linguistic evidence of ancient Eastern Cushites in East Africa south of the dry north of Kenya.[5] Even there the Eastern Cushitic Galla and Somali populations are products of movements of the last thousand years;[6] and while the Yaaku (Mokokodo) may have lived much longer in Kenya, their language does not appear to be the source of the Eastern Cushitic loanwords in Southern Nilotic.[7] If the area of contact is then to be placed to the north, the contacts must have preceded the Southern Nilotic settlement southward into East Africa because otherwise an unlikely history must be assumed, namely, that the pre–Southern Nilotes spread into East Africa, where they encountered the Southern Cushites, then spread back north to fall under overwhelming Eastern Cushitic influence, and finally spread south again to the very same areas where earlier they had met the Southern Cushites—for these were the areas in which they lived at the close of pre–Southern Nilotic times.

The middle pre–Southern Nilotic period probably began a number of centuries before the late pre–Southern Nilotic era. The intensity of Southern Nilotic word-borrowing from Eastern Cushitic suggests sustained Eastern Cushitic dominance over a period of centuries. In this light the middle pre–Southern Nilotic period could hardly have begun later than the early part of the first millennium B.C. even if late pre–Southern Nilotic times began very

3. See Chapter 2.

4. Harold Fleming, "Baiso and Rendille: Somali Outliers," *Rassegna di Studi Etiopici*, XX (1964).

5. The possibility of Eastern Cushite–Southern Nilote contacts in more southerly areas cannot be completely ruled out because this evidence, after all, is negative.

6. Fleming, *op. cit.*, and Herbert Lewis, "The Origins of the Galla and Somali," *Journal of African History*, VII (1966).

7. See Appendix B.1.

late in the same millennium; and it could have begun much earlier, in the second millennium, if the Southern Nilotes were already present in East Africa as early as the date of the Njoro River Cave site.

THE EARLY PRE–SOUTHERN NILOTES

The early pre–Southern Nilotic period must be seen for what it is, a catchall for whatever happened to the Southern Nilotes between the breakup of the proto-Nilotic community and the rise to importance of the Eastern Cushites. For now, there is little to be caught. The cultural contribution of the proto-Nilotes may have been carried on with little change by the early pre–Southern Nilotes, but only a little can as yet be said about what that culture was. Some suggestions, but suggestions only, can also be made about the early pre–Southern Nilotes' contacts with other peoples.

Although little can be said about early pre–Southern Nilotic culture, some of what can be said is extremely interesting: that already in proto-Nilotic times the Nilotes knew of and kept livestock. Words in Southern Nilotic for "cow," "goat," and "to herd" all appear to go back to proto-Nilotic.[8] The early pre–Southern Nilotes can be said, then, to have been from the start food-producers in economy, at least to the extent that they herded livestock. Unfortunately there is as yet no certain evidence as to whether the earliest pre–Southern Nilotes milked or bled their cattle; there is also as yet no linguistic evidence to demonstrate that they practiced any cultivation. More likely than not they already cultivated sorghum and perhaps other grains. Yet it is possible that they practiced mixed herding and hunting-gathering rather than mixed farming.

Ethnographical evidence can suggest other probable pre–Southern Nilotic culture features that would have been brought over from proto-Nilotic into early pre–Southern Nilotic times. Lack of hereditary chiefship, some sort of noncycling age-set organization, and a settlement pattern of individual family homesteads seem probable from the prevalence of these traits among the diverse Nilotic groups today. The extraction of the lower incisor teeth of adolescents was certainly practiced; it is very old among peoples of the eastern Sudan regions[9] and is still practiced generally by Nilotes today, even by those who also have adopted circumcision of adolescents from the Cushites. There

8. See Appendix A.2.
9. G. P. Murdock, *Africa: Its Peoples and Their Culture History* (New York: McGraw-Hill Book Co., 1959), pp. 155, 173, 337.

was surely no prohibition against women having contact with cattle,[10] although herding was probably an activity of boys and young men, as it normally is among Nilotes today. In many respects the culture of the proto-Nilotes and the early pre–Southern Nilotes appears to have been not unlike that of some of the modern Nilotes of northern Uganda and northern Kenya.

Locating the early pre–Southern Nilotic community rests largely on giving location to the proto-Nilotic community. On the grounds of geographical distribution of modern Nilotic languages, the land of the proto-Nilotes is probably to be placed in the lower dry regions to the west and southwest of the southern Ethiopian highlands. The old center of Western Nilotic settlement lay in the west parts of this area near the Nile River, a conclusion required by the distribution of the modern Western Nilotic languages. The Dinka and Nuer, whose languages form one subgroup of Western Nilotic, live on the Nile near the Bahr al-Ghazal confluence. The Luo peoples, whose languages form a second subgroup, live scattered on all sides of the Dinka-Nuer territory.[11] The Burun dialects, the third Western Nilotic subgroup, are spoken just northeast of the Dinka-Nuer region, still in the Sudan country below the Ethiopian plateau. The Eastern Nilotic homeland lay nearer Lake Rudolf and the southern Ethiopian highlands, probably in the countries westward from Lake Rudolf. Most of the Eastern Nilotes today are found between Lake Rudolf and the Nile, although one subgroup, Masaian, is spoken from northern Kenya south even into Tanzania. The late pre–Southern Nilotes and the proto–Southern Nilotes lived in western and southern Kenya,[12] but, as indicated, in earlier middle pre–Southern Nilotic times they very probably lived at least somewhat further north.[13] The over-all distribution of Nilotic languages in earlier times thus suggests the proto-Nilotic homeland as falling in a broad belt of territory running from northern Kenya and the Lake Rudolf region west and northwest toward the Nile River. The early pre–Southern Nilotes probably represent the evolving population of the easterly extension of this belt, with the ancient Eastern and Western Nilotic communities developing to the west and northwest of them

10. The practice of separating women from contact with cattle has been adopted in more recent times by the Luo, apparently from Central Sudanic peoples. For discussion see Murdock *op. cit.*, p. 228, and C. Ehret, "Sheep and Central Sudanic Peoples in Southern Africa,", *Journal of African History*, IX (1968).

11. Luo settlement in some parts of Uganda and in Kenya are the historically recent results of southward expansion.

12. See below, Chapter 5.

13. See above, p. 33.

(see Map 4).[14] To the north the pre–Southern Nilotes would have had as neighbors the early Eastern Cushitic peoples of the southern and southeastern Ethiopian highland fringes. A location in this general area would fit well climatically with postulation of cattle-keeping for the early pre–Southern Nilotes; it would also allow simple explanation of the presence of Eastern Cushitic influences, which become so important in the succeeding middle pre–Southern Nilotic era of Southern Nilotic history.

THE MIDDLE PRE–SOUTHERN NILOTES

The extraordinary impact of Eastern Cushitic dominance in the middle pre–Southern Nilotic period brought major new developments in Southern Nilotic culture. Under Eastern Cushitic influence the Southern Nilotes took over circumcision and clitoridectomy, practices general among the Cushites but not at that period practiced by any other Nilotes. The old Southern Nilotic verb for circumcision is even an originally Eastern Cushitic word. The Southern Nilotes also took over the Cushitic prohibition against eating fish, and they probably borrowed the idea of a cycling age-set system[15] from the Eastern Cushites at the same period. Linear age-set systems are common among the Nilotes and some of their neighbors, but the particular cycling kind of age system is unique to the Southern Nilotes and Eastern Cushites and therefore betokens the special contacts between the two peoples.

Southern Nilotic vocabulary-borrowings from Eastern Cushitic only emphasize the scale of Eastern Cushitic impact on the middle pre–Southern Nilotes. The Eastern Cushitic loanwords in Southern Nilotic include several basic words, even the word for "head," as well as words for the numbers 6 through 10 and for 20, 30, 40, and so on up to 100. Besides these, a goodly number of Eastern Cushitic loanwords can still easily be identified in other nonbasic parts of Southern Nilotic vocabulary.[16] Comparison with the East African situations where similarly heavy borrowing has occurred would

14. In view of the tendency of maps to convey an impression of precision in their representations of geography, it seems worthwhile to emphasize that Maps 4–9 do not claim to give more than the *probable approximate* locations of peoples in earlier times.

15. In a cycling system there is an established, limited set of names which are given in regular order to each successive initiation grouping. After the last name has been applied, the first name is used for the next grouping of initiates, followed by the second name, and so on through the cycle again. The Kalenjin system originally consisted of eight age-set names, each set including all those initiated over a period of approximately fifteen years. It took about 120 years to go through the whole cycle of names.

16. See Appendix B.1.

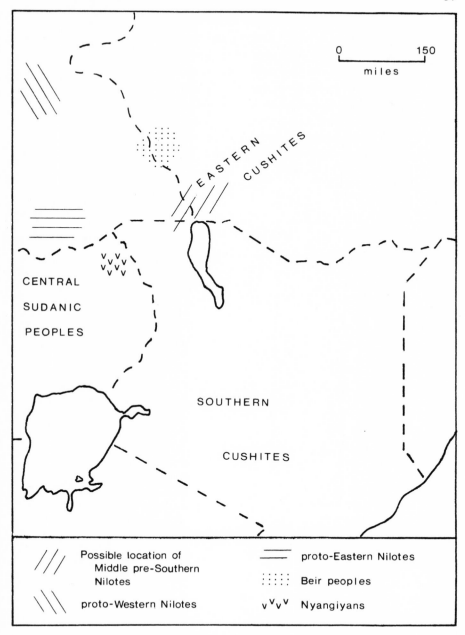

MAP 4. The Southern Nilotes, ca. 1000 B.C.

suggest that the middle pre–Southern Nilotes can hardly have been in any more favorable position with respect to the Eastern Cushites than many Dorobo peoples are today with respect to the dominant Masai. Nevertheless, the middle pre–Southern Nilotes must have maintained some degree of independence because they were never finally absorbed into the Eastern Cushitic populations of south Ethiopia and adjoining Kenya but instead were themselves able eventually to expand southward into East Africa and become a major force in the historical developments there. Perhaps a long-sustained contact of many centuries with the Eastern Cushites would explain the apparent intensity of word-borrowing.

What must be emphasized is that these Cushitic contacts affected only the Southern Nilotes. The Southern Nilotes have often been grouped with the Eastern Nilotes as "Nilo-Hamites," the "Hamite" half of the name meaning the Eastern Cushites and the whole name connoting a supposed common Cushitic element in both Nilotic peoples. This grouping is not justified historically, let alone linguistically.[17] Between Eastern Cushites and at least some of the Eastern Nilotes there have been contacts which have resulted in Eastern Nilotic word-borrowings from the Cushites. But these contacts were independent of the Southern Nilotic contacts with the Eastern Cushites and were nowhere nearly so strong or sustained as the contacts of the Southern Nilotes. What has further contributed to the Nilo-Hamitic idea is that within the Christian era several Eastern Nilotic peoples have come under the influence of Southern Nilotic peoples. This contact has meant in the case of the Masai, for instance, that the Masai have borrowed many words from Southern Nilotic languages, including a few words earlier borrowed by the Southern Nilotes from Cushitic. They have also borrowed circumcision from the Southern Nilotes,[18] who themselves had borrowed it from the Eastern Cushites.

17. For the linguistic statement see J. H. Greenberg, *The Languages of Africa* (Bloomington: Indiana University Research Center in Anthropology, Folklore, and Linguistics, 1963), pp. 85–108.
18. See below, Chapter 6.

CHAPTER 5

The Southern Nilotic Settlement
in East Africa

THE CONTEXT OF SETTLEMENT

The opening of the late pre–Southern Nilotic period was marked by the shift of the center of Southern Nilotic population from areas where Ethiopian contacts were the important external influence on their history to the general region of the rift valley and the western highlands in Kenya, where the Southern Nilotes first encountered the Southern Cushites. It is, in fact, the evidence of Southern Cushitic contacts that places the late pre–Southern Nilotic settlement in those parts of Kenya. The particular Southern Cushites who influenced the Southern Nilotes probably spoke a Rift Southern Cushitic language[1] and seem to have been, from certain sound characteristics of their language, the same people who later influenced the ancestors of the Kalenjin in the periods following the breakup of the proto–Southern Nilotic people.[2] A closely related language appears also to be the source of Southern Cushitic loanwords in Gusii.[3] The common factor in the histories of the Kalenjin and Gusii is their settlement in the western highlands, and so the common Southern Cushitic contacts of those histories would place the Southern Cushites encountered in the same general regions. If these Southern Cushites affected late pre–Southern Nilotic history as well, then late pre–Southern Nilotic country must likewise have been somewhere in the western highlands and rift-valley areas.

At least by the close of the late pre–Southern Nilotic period the Southern Nilotes were also in contact with Bantu-speaking people.[4] Presumably, Bantu penetration was from the south. To the north the Southern Nilotes seem to have shared in cultural developments with the Eastern Nilotes. The two share, for instance, the words "cow's hump" and "to forge iron."[5] The

1. Rift is one of three subgroups into which Southern Cushitic can be divided. Modern Rift languages are Iraqw, Burungi, Alagwa, Aramanik, and Ngomvia.
2. See Appendixes B.2 and B.3.
3. See Appendix B.5.
4. See Appendix E.1.
5. Compare proto-Southern *yu:k from pre–Southern Nilotic *riu:k, "cow's hump," with proto–Teso-Masaian *-rʋk, and proto–Southern Nilotic *tɔ:ny, "to forge," and proto–Teso-Masaian *-(i)doŋ.

introduction of humped cattle and iron-working must each have been con-
nected developments in the two areas.

The developing Southern Nilotic populations of the late pre–Southern Nilotic
period should be viewed as a collection of peoples speaking several closely
related dialects. Among these was the dialect, or group of especially closely
related dialects, from which the proto–Southern Nilotic speech derived. Only
descendant languages of proto–Southern Nilotic are still spoken today, but
there were a number of other Southern Nilotic dialects contemporary with
proto–Southern Nilotic which have left no modern descendant languages
(see Appendix A.7). The most clearly attested of peoples speaking such
dialects lived somewhere eastward from the shores of Lake Victoria and south
of the Kavirondo Gulf. Other dialects were spoken in central southern
Kenya and the neighboring Kilimanjaro areas. Still other pre–Southern
Nilotes may have lived on the plains and grasslands stretching between
Kilimanjaro and Lake Victoria (see Map 5). The dialect or dialects ancestral
to proto–Southern Nilotic were probably spoken north of this belt of territory,
because all the attested Southern Nilotic languages of more northerly areas in
later times show the defining sound change of proto–Southern Nilotic—the
loss of *r* before *i* in word-final syllables—or on other grounds can be shown to
descend from proto–Southern Nilotic.

The Victoria pre–Southern Nilotic population remained important for
many centuries in the areas east and southeast from Lake Victoria. They were
in the territory at least as early as the earliest Bantu, who, as indicated, were
already neighbors of Southern Nilotes before the end of the late pre–Southern
Nilotic period; they continued to inhabit parts of the country perhaps as late
as the present millennium before finally being absorbed by the Bantu. Their
presence is reflected in such culture traits as the cycling age-set systems of the
Kuria, Zanaki, and others of the region. It is still more evident in the numerous Southern Nilotic loanwords in Gusii and the Bantu dialects of the Musoma
and Mara areas especially and also in the various Gishu and Luhyia dialects.

Several pre–Southern Nilotic loanword strata in these Bantu languages can
be distinguished. One consists of a set of pre–Southern Nilotic words which
occur in all or nearly all the Bantu languages of the east shore of Lake
Victoria;[6] others consist of loanwords found in all the Bantu languages spoken

6. See Appendix D.1.

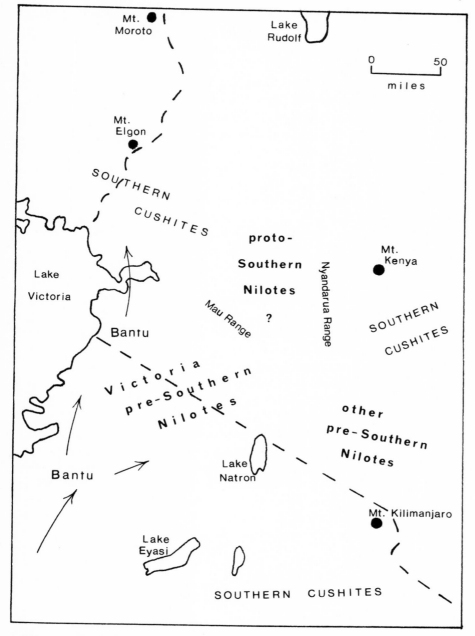

MAP 5.   The Proto–Southern Nilotes and Their Neighbors, ca. 100–400 A.D.

south of the Kavirondo Gulf or, in the case of some loanwords, in only one or a few of the Bantu dialects spoken in that region.[7] The strata can all be attributed to the same general source because certain phonetic characteristics are shared among them, such as retention of *r* before *i* in final syllables and the frequent correspondence of proto–Southern Nilotic *t* with *s* in loanwords in Bantu. No such stratum, however, is limited to the Luhyia and Gishu dialects alone. The clear implication is that the earliest contact between the Bantu and the Victoria Southern Nilotes occurred when the ancestors in language of all the Bantu of the east shore of Lake Victoria, from the Jita in the south to the Gishu in the north, were still close enough linguistically and geographically to share in the same word-borrowing. That is, the contact began with the beginning of settlement and differentiation among the Bantu on the east of Lake Victoria.

These ancestral East Victoria Bantu would best be seen as a collection of several small communities which spoke different, though still mutually intelligible, dialects of Bantu and which at about the same time began settling here and there through the country of the more mobile, more pastoral Victoria Southern Nilotes.[8] The proximity of the Bantu communities to one another and their continuing close contacts would have assured their sharing in influences and word-borrowing from the surrounding Southern Nilotes, whereas their separation into several groups would have allowed for the occasional variant forms of the Victoria Southern Nilotic loanwords that appear in modern Bantu languages of the eastern Lake Victoria shore.

The contacts between the pre–Southern Nilotes and the ancestors of the Kisii-, Mara-, and Musoma-area Bantu continued till long after the ancestors of the Luhyia and Gishu had ceased to participate in the contacts, presumably because they spread northward out of the area of contact. Determining just how long the contacts continued will require better knowledge of the numerous Bantu dialects of the Mara and Musoma areas of Tanzania, but it appears that several loanwords from Victoria Southern Nilotic may be limited to a very few dialects indeed. If so, Victoria Southern Nilotes could have continued to live in the area even into the present millennium.

7. See Appendixes D.2, D.3, and D.4.
8. The same sort of scattered Bantu settlement in agriculturally favorable areas was proceeding all across northern and central East Africa at that period, i.e., the beginning of Christian times. The situation of the modern Sonjo, located in several settlements scattered through Masai-controlled country, probably resembles that of the early Bantu settlers of the northern half of East Africa.

Some at least of the pre–Southern Nilotic peoples who settled in central southern Kenya probably also continued to exist into fairly recent times. Among the Bantu-speaking Thagicu group of peoples, a few Southern Nilotic loanwords go back to proto-Thagicu, as their attestation in both Kikuyu and Kamba indicates, while other such words apparently occur in one descendant language, Kikuyu, and are therefore more recently borrowed.[9] The long continuation of Southern Nilotic presence in the region is also suggested by loanword evidence in the Masaian languages. Southern Nilotic contacts began for the Masaian peoples in the proto-Masaian period;[10] separate contacts affected Ongamo history subsequent to the breakup of the proto–Masaian community.[11]

The words of the various pre–Southern Nilotic loanword sets in the modern languages of central southern Kenya and the Kilimanjaro area lack special characteristics which identify them as all coming from the same source language. It is very likely that several separate Southern Nilotic peoples interacted with the various Bantu and Masaian peoples who successively assimilated them over the past two millennia. Certainly, over the long period of time involved, dialect differences would have evolved among the Southern Nilotes of different parts of the region even if originally only one pre–Southern Nilotic people had settled there.

That pre–Southern Nilotes spread also across parts of the plains between Lake Victoria and the Kilimanjaro region seems likely, but loanword evidence for such a settlement is harder to come by. The reason is that later immigrants into the region, the Dadog in the first millennium A.D. and the South Kalenjin in this millennium, were also Southern Nilotic–speakers, and loanwords from one Southern Nilotic language to another, such as from the speech of the pre–Southern Nilotes into that of their Dadog successors, are difficult to distinguish from older common Southern Nilotic words. The only lasting non-Nilotic presence in the area has been that of the Bantu Sonjo. And the Sonjo language does indeed contain a number of words which appear to attest contact of the ancestors of the Sonjo with pre–Southern Nilotes.[12]

9. See Appendix D.6. Better knowledge of other Thagicu vocabularies, especially of Meru spoken north of Kikuyu, would allow a more detailed and perhaps otherwise modified statement of the history of these contacts.

10. See Appendix F.2.

11. See Appendix F.4.

12. See Appendix D.7. In addition to these loanwords unique to Sonjo, and therefore attesting contacts unique to Bantu-speaking ancestors of the Sonjo, there are as many Southern Nilotic loanwords in Sonjo which it shares either with the Southeast Victoria Bantu

Still another Southern Nilotic people, apparently pre–Southern Nilotic in speech, lived as far south as west central Tanzania. A few words from a Southern Nilotic language appear in Gogo, Nyamwezi, Sangu, and other neighboring Bantu languages.[13] As yet this loanword material is too sparse and scattered in attestation to allow anything specific to be said about the Southern Nilotic role in that area.

LATE PRE–SOUTHERN NILOTIC CULTURE

The pre–Southern Nilotes who were spread over so large an area of East Africa at the beginning of the Christian era were both herders and cultivators. As vocabulary attributable to late pre–Southern Nilotic indicates,[14] they kept cattle including humped breeds, goats, and donkeys.[15] They branded their cattle, and they knew of at least two East African grains, sorghum and eleusine. Evidence is lacking, however, that they planted either bananas or root crops.

By the end of late pre–Southern Nilotic times they knew of iron, but it seems improbable that they ever made use of the iron hoe. In fact, iron hoes may not have come into general use among Southern Nilotes until as late as the present millennium. The evidence for this proposition is negative, but strikingly negative. There is no common Southern Nilotic word and, moreover, not even a common Kalenjin word for "hoe." There are, instead, at least four unrelated roots in Southern Nilotic for "hoe," all of them loanwords and all but one of them from a Bantu language.[16] The unanimity of the evidence points strongly to the conclusion that the iron hoe is in every case a

languages or with Kikuyu. Either Sonjo has borrowed the words from its Bantu relatives in one or both cases, or the ancestors of the Sonjo could have participated in the same contacts with Southern Nilotes as either the Southeast Victoria Bantu or the Kikuyu and therefore have been influenced to borrow many of the same words.

13. See Appendix D.8. Whether yet other early Southern Nilotic populations existed in East Africa is not known. One piece of evidence does suggest an area for possible further investigation: the word *-moori, "calf" or "heifer," related to proto–Southern Nilotic *mɔːi < pre–Southern Nilotic *mɔːri, "calf," is found not only in all East Victoria Bantu dialects and in Thagicu languages but also in Shambala, Zigula, and Swahili. But if Southern Nilotes did indeed directly influence the ancestors of these three Bantu peoples or others among the far northeastern Bantu, that influence is not easily detectable in their languages.

14. For late pre–Southern Nilotic economic vocabulary see Appendix A.3.

15. No doubt they kept sheep also, because sheep were known in East Africa in earlier times and were certainly kept by their immediate descendants, the proto–Southern Nilotes; but the attribution of a word for "sheep" to the pre–Southern Nilotic vocabulary cannot yet be made.

16. See Appendixes E.3, E.4, E.6, and G.1.

relatively recent adoption by the Southern Nilotes and that in most cases the means of introduction were Bantu peoples.

The late pre–Southern Nilotes certainly collected honey and presumably they made honey wine from it, as their proto–Southern Nilotic descendants did. From the incoming Bantu they appear to have borrowed a new kind of man-made beehive. Among the words they borrowed from Bantu was *mori:ŋ(k)-, "beehive," which in later proto–Southern Nilotic became *moi:ŋ(k)-.[17] The Rift Southern Cushites also widely borrowed this Bantu word; Iraqw has, for example, miringamo and Aramanik has meringo. Honey-collecting is an old, even preagricultural, practice in East Africa, and so the adoption of the practice is not the reason for the widespread borrowing of the word for "beehive." Instead the likely reason is that the spread of the name was associated with the spread of the common modern East African form of man-made beehive, the "honey barrel." The Bantu should be credited with its introduction into East Africa.

The late pre–Southern Nilotic societies, like recent Kalenjin societies, were organized around cycling age-set systems. It appears likely that five and perhaps six of the eight pre–Southern Nilotic age-set names and their order in the cycle can still be determined: (1) *sɔ:e, (2) *gorongoro, (3) unknown, (4) *gini (?), (5) unknown, (6) *nyangi or *nyɔ:ngi, (7) *maina, (8) *cu:ma. The basis of determination is the occurrence among the Kuria and several other Bantu peoples of the area southeast of Lake Victoria of cycling age-set systems with eight age sets in the whole cycle, just as formerly was the case among the Kalenjin.[18] The first two and last three names occur in both Kalenjin and Kuria cycles and in exactly the same positions in the cycles. The five names, it should be noted, are each of two syllables[19] and are underivable from other Southern Nilotic or Bantu words. The name gini, for the second set after *gorongoro and the second set before *nyangi in the age-set systems of the Kuria and other Bantu of the southeast Victoria region, has been suggested as a sixth ancient Southern Nilotic age-set name because it shares these same two characteristics. The remaining age-set names in both Kalenjin and Bantu cycles appear to be words coined at some later date,[20]

17. See Appendix E.1.

18. Among some Kalenjin one of the original eight Kalenjin sets has dropped out of use. For comparison of Kuria and Kalenjin cycles see Appendix A.4.

19. *Gorongoro is a reduplicated form of a two-syllable stem *goro.

20. The other Kuria names, nyambureti and gamunyere, have the prefixes nya- and ga-, whose normal use in Kuria is to form nouns derived from other words in the language. The other Kalenjin names also have prefixes and suffixes showing they are late, derived forms; e.g., Kalenjin *kaple:lac can be interpreted as "group of the white ones."

presumably replacing earlier names. The Kuria age-set names do not come from a Kalenjin source; this is apparent from the quite different shapes of some of the names. For example, proto-Kalenjin had *sɔːwe where Kuria has saai, and *nyɔːnki where Kuria has nyangi. Outside of recent nearby Kalenjin peoples, the only Southern Nilotes known to have lived in the region are the Victoria Southern Nilotes. Most probably, then, the Kuria age-set system was borrowed from Victoria Southern Nilotes; and since the Victoria Southern Nilotes came into existence in late pre–Southern Nilotic times, the reconstructed age-set names go back to that period.

How political power was distributed in pre–Southern Nilotic societies is not explicit in the linguistic evidence. The ethnographic comparison of the modern Southern Nilotic societies and those, such as the Kuria, strongly influenced by the Southern Nilotes suggests that the younger, generally un-married men were the warriors of the community, while the opinions and personalities of older, married men had the greater influence on decision-making in the society. The age distinction in social roles was probably marked by separate names for the two different age grades, but there is little sugges-tion from Southern Nilotic practices that the Southern Nilotes themselves ever had any really elaborate age-grading systems such as operated among the Galla and some of the northeast coastal Bantu of Kenya.

THE END OF LATE PRE–SOUTHERN NILOTIC TIMES

The late pre–Southern Nilotic period ended with the development of the proto–Southern Nilotic community out of the late pre–Southern Nilotic populations of Kenya. With this development the momentum of Southern Nilotic change and expansion began to shift to the proto–Southern Nilotes and their descendants, and an era in the settlement of East Africa was brought to a close.

On the whole, proto–Southern Nilotes behaved and worked not much differently from the pre–Southern Nilotes of the end of pre–Southern Nilotic times. They kept cattle, planted grains, knew and used iron, and maintained the Southern Nilotic cycling age-set system. Sometimes it is possible, however, to credit the proto–Southern Nilotes with the use of items which may well have been known to pre–Southern Nilotes but which cannot be shown certainly to have been known to them. There were, that is, proto–Southern Nilotic words for the items, but the words cannot be shown to have been in Southern Nilotic languages before the proto–Southern Nilotic period.[21] The proto–Southern Nilotes had, among other such items, the large oval shield still used today, cowries, copper for rings, pots, and at least one kind of leather sack. In their subsistence practices they made use of their cattle's blood: there was a proto–Southern Nilotic word for the special kind of arrow used to bleed cattle. From general considerations of the wide East African spread of the trait of bleeding cattle, one would expect that the earlier pre–Southern Nilotes also consumed cow's blood, but no words dealing with the practice can yet be attributed to pre–Southern Nilotic dialects.

Other Southern Nilotes continued for a long time to live in parts of southern Kenya and northern Tanzania, their territories successively shrinking before encroaching Bantu and Eastern Nilotes. But the threads of cultural development which lead from pre–Southern Nilotic times down to the present passed through the weave of proto–Southern Nilotic culture. It was the descendants of the proto–Southern Nilotes—the Kalenjin, the Kitoki[22] Southern Nilotes, the Kenya-Kadam peoples, and the Dadog—who participated in the large population movements of the centuries since the end of the pre–Southern Nilotic period, and it is the Kalenjin and Dadog whose languages are still spoken today. And even as the brief proto–Southern Nilotic period marked the end of an era of settlement, so it signaled the opening of a new era, where the chief competitors of the Southern Nilotes would be, no longer Southern Cushites, but Eastern Nilotes and Bantu.

21. See Appendix A.3.

22. A name for the Bukusu occurring in several versions in Kony (Kalenjin), Idakho (Bantu), and other nearby dialects can in each case be seen to go back to an original form *Kitoki. The name is not used by the Bukusu to describe themselves, nor is it a Bantu word in origin (initial ki- here is probably the Nilotic prefix); and it is not a readily apparent descriptive name applicable to the Bukusu. It would thus best be interpreted as a relatively old coinage and, in that case, as originally referring to an earlier people than the Bukusu; cf. -tatua, p. 56. *Kitoki is therefore free to be used as a name for the Kitoki Southern Nilotes, since it probably earlier did name a people of the country south of Mount Elgon today inhabited by Bukusu, and a Kitoki Southern Nilotic people did interact with the ancestors of the Bukusu, probably in that area.

CHAPTER 6

Southern Nilotes in Kenya in the First Millennium A.D.

Between the end of the proto–Southern Nilotic period and the end of the proto-Kalenjin period, a span of time running from the first half of the first millennium A.D. to the early part of the present millennium, Southern Nilotes came finally to replace the Southern Cushites as the dominant peoples of western and central Kenya. Not only did the ancestors of the Kalenjin expand in the western highlands, at the expense, apparently, of Southern Cushites, but other descendants of the proto–Southern Nilotes came to control large areas of central and northern Kenya, from the rift valley to the plains of central eastern Uganda (see Map 6). Their presence is reflected in Southern Nilotic loanword sets in Bantu languages, in Tepeth and Yaaku, and in some of the Eastern Nilotic languages.

SOUTHERN NILOTES IN THE WESTERN HIGHLANDS

As indicated in the preceding chapter, the ancestral Kalenjin people renewed or maintained contact with many of the same Southern Cushites as their pre–Southern Nilotic predecessors. These Southern Cushites spoke a language of the Rift group and lived in western Kenya. The proto-Kalenjin vocabulary contained a goodly number of loans from Rift Cushitic, which occur in many parts of Kalenjin vocabulary, ranging from words for implements and adornment to wild animals and agriculture.[1] The Rift peoples may have held a general cultural dominance over the ancestors of the Kalenjin during parts of the first millennium; on the other hand, the Southern Cushitic loanwords in Kalenjin more probably represent the contribution of the Cushites to the Kalenjin peoples who in time absorbed them. Whether or not there may have been a time in the first millennium when the Kalenjin held a subordinate role in western Kenya, by the end of the proto-Kalenjin period Southern Cushitic importance there had certainly declined, for it is difficult to date any Southern Cushitic loanwords in Kalenjin dialects as definitely borrowed after the proto-Kalenjin period.[2]

1. See Appendix B.3.
2. See below, Chapter 8.

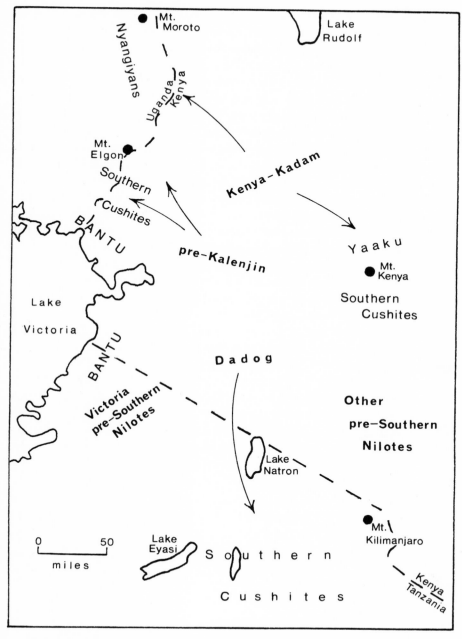

MAP 6. Directions of Southern Nilotic Expansion, ca. 400–1000 A.D.

But the ancestors of the Kalenjin not only came into contact with Southern Cushites; they also were influenced by at least one Bantu-speaking people. Bantu influences are manifested predominantly in the agricultural and food-preparation vocabularies. Apparently the Kalenjin looked to their Bantu neighbors for ideas in agriculture but otherwise were little influenced by them. Some of the Bantu loanwords may have come into Kalenjin as the names of newly introduced implements or foods. An example is the large spoon of the type called *mwiko* in Swahili, which may not have been used before by Southern Nilotes.[3] Other loanwords may simply attest Bantu importance in the western Kenyan agriculture of the time. The proto-Kalenjin word for "flour," for instance, was borrowed from Bantu, but surely the grain-cultivating Southern Nilotes must already have known of flour. The particular Bantu language which gave the words to proto-Kalenjin appears to have been most closely related to the modern Luhyia and Gishu dialects, but it seems to stand in a group by itself among these dialects.[4] It was very probably spoken in the country west of the Uasin Gishu plains and southeast of Mount Elgon because a Bantu people speaking what appears to have been the same language exerted especially strong influences on the Kony people who settled in that area in much later times.[5]

By the end of the first millennium other Southern Nilotic groups were established in the areas between the Kavirondo Gulf and Mount Elgon. These Kitoki Southern Nilotes do not seem to have been Kalenjin, but, if they were not Kalenjin, their language nevertheless seems to have been very closely related to proto-Kalenjin (see Appendix A.7). Most of the Kitoki Southern Nilotic loanwords in Luhyia and Gishu are today found only in Kalenjin dialects among the Southern Nilotic languages, and few if any are found only in Dadog. On the other hand, there are enough differences in the forms of some of the Kitoki Southern Nilotic loanwords to suggest that Kitoki Southern Nilotic was not identical with proto-Kalenjin.[6] So closely related to the proto-Kalenjin in language, the Kitoki Southern Nilotes could only have split off from the ancestors of the Kalenjin late in the first millennium A.D., not long before the proto-Kalenjin period. The Kitoki Southern

---

3. There is no proto–Southern Nilotic word for this implement. Both Southern Nilotic branches, Kalenjin and Dadog, have borrowed their words independently from different Bantu languages, a situation suggesting that the implement was a Bantu innovation.
4. See Appendix E.2.
5. See Appendix E.3.
6. See Appendixes D.9, D.10, and D.11.

Nilotes should be seen as representing the westward extension of the same population movements which brought the Kalenjin proper to a predominant position in the western highlands by the beginning of the present millennium.

THE KENYA-KADAM PEOPLES

In the lower country northward from the early ancestors of the Kalenjin lived another Southern Nilotic people, whose country at its greatest extent probably reached from the areas near Mount Kenya to the plains of central eastern Uganda north of Mount Elgon and around Mount Kadam. They may be called the Kenya-Kadam people after the large mountains at each extreme of their territory. The Kenya-Kadam people spoke a language probably more closely related to Kalenjin than to Dadog but not nearly so closely related as Kitoki Southern Nilotic to Kalenjin (see Appendix A.7).

Their language has left loanwords in at least two modern non–Southern Nilotic languages of East Africa, Tepeth, spoken on Mount Kadam and Mount Moroto in eastern Uganda, and Yaaku, otherwise known as Mokokodo, spoken in Kenya just north of Mount Kenya. The Southern Nilotic loanwords in the two languages can be attributed to the same source because they share a number of common phonological and semantic developments. For example, Southern Nilotic vowel sequences *oi and *ui between consonants become simply o or u; some Southern Nilotic *e's become *i's; and some Southern Nilotic *a:'s become ɔ's.[7] Both Tepeth and Yaaku have also borrowed a loanword with the particular stem shape -pon- and the particular meaning "oribi," different in both sound and meaning from the apparent Kalenjin cognate *po:in-, "bushbuck." On the other hand, quite distinct dialects of the Kenya-Kadam language must have come to be spoken at the two ends of the Kenya-Kadam country. This conclusion is required by the very different shapes of the loanword for "oribi" in Tepeth and Yaaku. The Tepeth form is *ponot*, while the Yaaku form is *kiponi*.

For both the Yaaku and the Tepeth, their early contacts with the Kenya-Kadam people must have been a major influence on their histories. In Yaaku a fair number of Southern Nilotic loanwords are still evident despite massive replacement of older Yaaku words by very recent loanwords from Masai. Even the name they call themselves by, *Yaaku*, was originally a Kenya-

7. For further examples and for Kenya-Kadam loanword lists see Appendixes H.1 and H.2.

Kadam loanword.[8] For the Tepeth of eastern Uganda, still stronger Southern
Nilotic dominance seems required by the number and penetration of Kenya-
Kadam loanwords in Tepeth vocabulary: even the words "chest" and "small"
come from Southern Nilotic. The situations of the Tepeth and Yaaku
peoples in the era of Kenya-Kadam contacts may not in fact have been much
different from what they were at the beginning of the twentieth century: both
peoples living in backwater areas and surrounded by other, dominant peoples.
In Tepeth history the Kenya-Kadam people played the same role as the later
Karamojong and Pokot; in Yaaku history, they played much the same role as
the later Masai.

The contact periods evidenced by the Kenya-Kadam loanwords in Tepeth
and Yaaku can be dated only very generally. It is probable that the Kenya-
Kadam language, from its proposed relationships with other Southern
Nilotic languages, evolved into a separate language in the course of the first
millennium A.D. It was considerably different from proto-Kalenjin, different
enough that it must have separated from ancestral Kalenjin speech a number
of centuries before the proto-Kalenjin period. Before the contacts reflected in
Yaaku and Tepeth vocabularies began, some centuries of separate evolution in
Kenya-Kadam must be allowed for development of the several distinctive
phonological features of the Kenya-Kadam language. Then still more time
should be allowed for the evident dialect differences to develop between the
Kenya-Kadam dialect that affected Tepeth and the dialect that affected
Yaaku. Thus, though the Kenya-Kadam people may have begun to develop a
separate identity as early as the middle of the first millennium, their expansion across the whole country between Mount Kadam and Mount Kenya
might not have been complete until very late in the millennium. Contacts
between the Kenya-Kadam people and the Tepeth and Yaaku could have
begun as early as the end of the first millennium, or they might not have
begun until sometime in the early centuries of the present millennium. Moreover, the Kenya-Kadam contacts with one of the two peoples might have
begun before the end of the first millennium while not beginning till later
with the other.

SOUTHERN NILOTES AND MASAIAN PEOPLES

At least two other early Southern Nilotic loanword strata in non–Southern
Nilotic languages derive from events of the first millennium A.D. in Kenya.

8. See Appendix H.2.

The loanword set of clearest historical implication consists of words reconstructible for proto-Masaian. The Southern Nilotic loanwords of the set include names for a number of important large wild animals and the words for "shield," "immature ewe," and "circumcision."[9] The Southern Nilotes whose words appear in proto-Masaian clearly had a heavy impact on the early Masaian people. What is especially significant is that the Masaian community apparently borrowed the practice of circumcision from them. It was apparently during the same period that the Masaian peoples adopted the long oval Southern Nilotic type of shield, because the proto-Masaian word for the item is a Southern Nilotic loanword. The Masaian community may well have adopted many other Southern Nilotic traits at this time, such as a prohibition against eating fish, spears with long narrow blades, and several items of dress.[10] Lacking corroborating linguistic evidence, the time of borrowing of these last traits cannot be finally determined; Masaian peoples, after all, continued in contact with various Southern Nilotes into much more recent times. But the trend toward cultural assimilation of the Masaian peoples by the Southern Nilotes who preceded them in southern Kenya certainly received strong impetus in this period.

The Southern Nilotes whose words appear in proto-Masaian are probably to be included among those whose existence as a separate people dates back to late pre–Southern Nilotic times. Most of the words in the loanword set can be reconstructed for proto–Southern Nilotic or pre–Southern Nilotic. The very few which today occur only in Kalenjin or only in Dadog could easily be words which are just as old in Southern Nilotic but happened to be retained in only one of the two branches of Southern Nilotic. Moreover, one word which may belong to the set retains the *r* lost in proto–Southern Nilotic.

The area of contact between these Southern Nilotes and the ancestral Masaian people was very possibly somewhere in the plains country between the Nyandarua Range and Kilimanjaro and east of the rift valley. At least the late proto-Masaian homeland is likely to have been in these general regions. Masai traditions suggest that Masai origins lie in Kenya, and the speakers of Masai's sister language, Ongamo, have long lived about Kilimanjaro. A proto-Masaian homeland between the Nyandarua Range and Kilimanjaro

9. See Appendix F.2.
10. For culture-sharings between Southern Nilotes and Masaian peoples see G. W. B. Huntingford, *The Southern Nilo-Hamites* (London: International African Institute, 1953), especially the charts on pp. 15 and 16. Huntingford's comparisons are specifically of Masai with Nandi but would work equally well with most of the other Southern Nilotic communities.

would allow neatly for the possibility of Ongamo expansion around Kilimanjaro and Masai expansion north and south along the plains of the neighboring
rift-valley region. Early widespread Masaian settlement in the area is required
in any case by the strong Masaian loanword strata in Chaga, Gweno, Taita,
and Kikuyu—Bantu languages spoken all about the area today.[11] If the
proto-Masaian peoples are to be seen as most likely settlers in the plains
between the Nyandarua Range and Kilimanjaro, then the Southern Nilotes
who affected them so strongly could well have been their neighbors and
predecessors there.

The other early Southern Nilotic loanword set that bears on developments
of the first millennium A.D. consists of a few words shared by Masaian,
Karamojong-Teso, and Lotuko, the languages which together constitute the
Teso-Masaian branch of Eastern Nilotic. The words were borrowed, that is,
at a time when proto–Teso-Masaian—the common ancestral language of the
Masaian, Karamojong-Teso, and Lotuko languages—was still spoken. The
contact period represented by the loanword set presumably had its setting in
northern Kenya or adjoining eastern Uganda since it happened when the
ancestors of the various Teso-Masaian groups were still one people or one
cluster of closely associated peoples. It is to be dated to the first millennium
A.D. because the particular Southern Nilotic people with which the proto–
Teso-Masaians interacted were descendants of the proto–Southern Nilotes.
There is some evidence that these Southern Nilotes may in fact have been a
branch of the Kenya-Kadam peoples, who spread so widely across eastern
Uganda and northern Kenya in the first millennium.[12]

With the breakup of the proto–Teso-Masaian community, the ancestors of
the Masaian peoples spread southward into central south Kenya, there to fall
under the influence, already described, of the Southern Nilotes of those
regions; but for the ancestors of the Karamojong-Teso and Lotuko communities, significant Southern Nilotic influence came to an end with their development into separate peoples.

11. For Masaian loanwords in Kikuyu see T. G. Benson, ed., *Kikuyu-English Dictionary*
(Oxford: Clarendon Press, 1964). For loanwords in the other languages see C. Ehret, *Ethiopians
and East Africans: The Problem of Contacts* (Nairobi: East African Publishing House, 1971),
Table 8-2. Masaian loans occur also in Asu (Pare).
12. See Appendix F.1.

CHAPTER 7

The Dadog

THE EMERGENCE AND EXPANSION OF THE DADOG

Even as the Southern Nilotic peoples of western and central Kenya were evolving their separate identities out of the breakup of the proto–Southern Nilotic community, the ancestors of the Dadog may have been spreading southward, eventually to occupy large parts of central northern Tanzania. Here their earlier presence is attested in such disparate languages as Sonjo, Iraqw, and Aramanik. Their earliest and most important settlement in Tanzania was in modern northern and central Masailand. Later expansion carried their speech southwestward into the present Mbulu and Singida areas, where most of the remaining Dadog peoples can be found today (see Map 7).

The old Dadog-speaking population of Masailand was in contact with early Sonjo and Aramanik peoples; its presence may also be reflected in Akie, the Kalenjin language of the so-called Dorobo of far southern Masailand.[1] The contacts differed in degree and kind and so give evidence of the differing situation of the Dadog people in different parts of their country.

The Dadog impact on the ancestors of the Sonjo seems to have been fairly heavy. Even the language of the dominant Masai, who surround the Sonjo today, has had a less penetrating effect on Sonjo vocabulary than did early Dadog. The evidence of Dadog contact would fit well with the idea that the Sonjo may even then have lived much as they do now, as isolated cultivators and Bantu-speakers surrounded by non-Bantu pastoral peoples. The dominance of the Dadog in matters of livestock-raising is seen in the derivation from Dadog of the Sonjo names for both "cattle fold" and "calf fold."

The Sonjo contacts may not have represented the western limit of the old Dadog population. A word in Gusii may just possibly also be from Dadog,[2] in which case some Dadog might have lived much farther west toward Lake

1. See Appendixes C.1, D.12, and H.3.
2. Gusii *-gos-, "to tan," compares with Dadog gu:š-, "to tan." If it is a loanword, for phonological reasons it would have to be borrowed from Dadog: Dadog š < *lʸ, and the Gusii form has s (for š, which Gusii lacks), reflecting the Dadog sound change.

55

Victoria, perhaps in the Mara area, where some Masai live today. However, one possible loanword is hardly sufficient evidence for even a tentative conclusion.

Whatever their eventual southward extension, the Dadog of the Masai steppe lived at least as far south as central Masailand. This presence is indicated in the vocabulary of Aramanik, the Southern Cushitic–speaking hunting peoples of the region. The ancestors of the Aramanik seem, in fact, to have come under Dadog domination much as the modern Aramanik are overshadowed by the Masai. The quality of the evidence for this view is what matters since the quantity of evidence is not great. It is not great simply because over-all knowledge of the Aramanik vocabulary is slight. The primary evidence is the number system. At one time probably all the numerals except one, two, four, and ten were borrowed from Dadog.[3] In all other instances in East Africa extensive borrowing in the number system has been accompanied by heavy borrowing in other parts of the vocabulary. Presumably, then, the same situation will be found true for Aramanik once its vocabulary is better known. If so, the Aramanik of earlier times should be viewed as hunters and gatherers living in an area settled also by a dominant and more numerous Dadog people, primarily herders in economy, a situation very like the situation of the Aramanik and the Masai today.

Some hint as to the antiquity of Dadog settlement in northern Tanzania is given by the apparent antiquity of *Dadog* as a name for the Dadog-speaking peoples. It already occurred in proto–West Rift in the form *Tara*, "Dadog."[4] The Dadog, then, appear to have lived continuously within areas well known to the West Rift Cushites since at least as early as the proto–West Rift period, a time probably in the first millennium A.D. The well-known area in earlier times was in all likelihood Masailand, where widespread Dadog settlement is clearly indicated. What is most interesting is that the Dadog have apparently been called by the same name since such a very early date.

Early though West Rift knowledge of Dadog peoples may be, the actual

---

3. In modern Aramanik the words for the numbers eight and nine are loanwords from Masai. It has been assumed here that the Masai loans replaced earlier words borrowed from Dadog because, in other cases, the words for eight and nine are usually borrowed if those for six and seven are.

4. The stem of *Dadog* is *dad-*. Another Dadog tribal name, for hunting peoples, *haged-*, also comes out in at least one West Rift language, Burungi, as *hagir-*, again with r for Dadog *d* at the end of the stem of a word. Apparently both *tara* and *hagir-* came into West Rift languages either directly from an extinct Dadog dialect which changed *d* to r or indirectly through an intermediate language in which the sound change occurred.

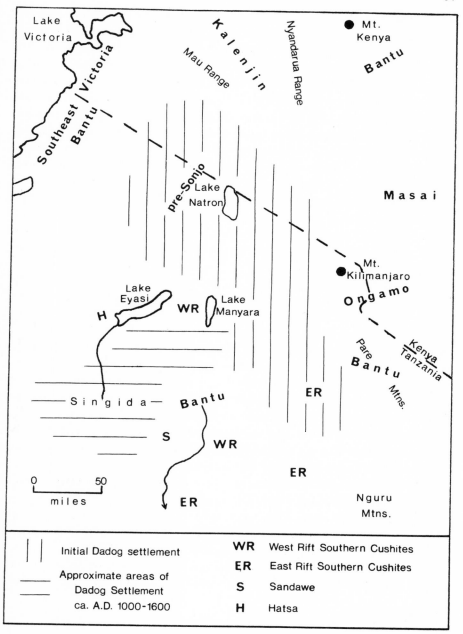

MAP 7. The Countries of Dadog History

penetration of the Dadog into the Rift Cushite–dominated highlands of
Mbulu and northern parts of Kondoa seems not to have begun until much
later—not at least until Iraqwan had become a language distinct from either
Burungi or Alagwa. The distinct existence of Iraqwan at the time of Dadog
settlement must be assumed because most of the numerous Southern Cushitic
loanwords in Dadog can be traced to a specifically Iraqwan source while none
can be attributed directly to Burungi or Alagwa.[5] It was Iraqwan peoples,
apparently, whose territories lay in the path of Dadog advance, whereas the
ancestors of the Burungi and Alagwa were not directly affected by the new
immigrants. This conclusion is bolstered by the striking lack of Dadog
loanwords not only in Burungi and apparently Alagwa but in neighboring
Bantu Irangi, in contrast to the clear occurrence of Dadog loanwords in Iraqw
and Gorowa, as well as other languages to the immediate west of Burungi and
Irangi.[6] Dadog expansion through Mbulu and Kondoa would seem to have
passed to the north and west of modern Irangi- and Burungi-speaking
country.

The southwestern advance of the Dadog eventually extended through the
Singida area. The Dadog may have preceded the Nyaturu in many parts of

Though the Dadog advance must be dated long enough after the breakup
of the proto–West Rift community for the early Iraqwan language to have
already developed characteristics of its own, it nevertheless began very early in
the history of the separate Iraqwan language. Some of the Southern Cushitic
loanwords may be recent loans from Iraqw or Gorowa, but others certainly
were borrowed long ago. One example is the Dadog word *sirbi:d*, "waterpot."
From its shape the word can only have come from Iraqwan; yet the Dadog
form maintains a *b* which had already changed to *w* in Iraqwan even before
Gorowa developed into a dialect separate from Iraqw. Although the word was
borrowed from Iraqwan, it had to have been borrowed in a relatively early
period. A different kind of example is *fayu:d*, Dadog for "arrow shaft." Today
the word is found among the West Rift languages only in Burungi and Alagwa,
but there the word has the meaning simply of "arrow." The Dadog form may
be from another now extinct West Rift language; but in view of the evidence
of words like *sirbi:d* a more likely interpretation is that the Dadog borrowing
is from an older Iraqwan form of the West Rift word, having its own characteristic meaning but no longer in use in modern Iraqw.

The southwestern advance of the Dadog eventually extended through the
Singida area. The Dadog may have preceded the Nyaturu in many parts of

5. See Appendix B.6.
6. See Appendixes C.2, D.13, H.5, and H.6.

the area, but neither people seems to have had overwhelming early impact on the other. A number of Dadog loanwords occur in Nyaturu, but not in any basic parts of the vocabulary.[7] Perhaps the Dadog should be seen as only sparsely occupying the area and already sharing the occupation of it with equally scattered Bantu-speaking ancestors of the Nyaturu. Heavy Dadog settlement in earlier times in the Iramba country north of the Nyaturu is not now required by the loanword evidence, although better knowledge of the Iramba dialects could possibly modify this picture.

THE DECLINE OF THE DADOG

The decline of Dadog influence in Masailand probably began even as Dadog expansion into Mbulu and Singida was still under way. The South Kalenjin people, who pushed into Tanzania between about five hundred and a thousand years ago,[8] initiated the Dadog decline. The Masai use of the tribal name *il-tatua* suggests that at the height of the South Kalenjin domination of Masailand the Dadog population may already have become restricted to the areas bordering Mbulu on the north and east, the areas around Lake Manyara. *Il-tatua* is used by the Masai to name two quite different peoples, the Bantu Mbugwe, who live just south of Lake Manyara, and the Southern Cushitic Iraqw, who live west and southwest from the Lake Manyara area. It consists of *tat-*, a form of the stem of the name *Dadog*, and an additional Southern Nilotic suffix *-ua*. The Masai have thus borrowed the name from a Southern Nilotic people, in all likelihood the South Kalenjin, because South Kalenjin had no *d* phoneme and would have replaced the *d*'s in **dad-* with their nearest equivalent sound, *t*. A likely explanation of the Masai usage is that the South Kalenjin called the Dadog by a name **tatua*, a form of the name *Dadog*, and that even after their expansion across northern Masailand they continued to use the name to refer to Dadog-speaking populations still in possession of country west and south of Lake Manyara. Their successors in Masailand, the Masai, borrowed this term; but between the South Kalenjin period and the present the Dadog language was replaced by Mbugwe in some places and Iraqw in others. Still, the Masai continued to refer to the people in the Manyara area indiscriminately by the old term even though the tribal configuration had completely changed.

Further south, in Mbulu, Singida, and parts of Kondoa, the tide of Dadog

7. See Appendix D.13.
8. See Chapter 9.

expansion crested late; and the ebb tide, the assimilation of the Dadog by surrounding peoples, began almost within reach of more traditional types of historical evidence, such as oral sources. It was signaled by new stirrings among the Iraqwan peoples of Mbulu, then probably relatively few in number and greatly restricted in territory by the earlier Dadog immigration. It received its first clear expression in the settlement of the ancestors of the Gorowa west of Mbulu in far northern Kondoa, an area probably Dadog in speech at the time.[9] The separation of the Gorowa from the Iraqw and their expansion into their present country probably occurred just a few hundred years ago. Its sequel is the late expansion of the Iraqw, an expansion which has spread Iraqw speech over much of Mbulu and which continues today at the expense of Dadog peoples of southern Mbulu. The Iraqw advance has been matched by the expansion of the Bantu Nyaturu northeastward into former Dadog speech areas of Singida, an expansion also apparently still under way.

Dadog history has come full circle, then. It began sometime in the first millennium A.D. with the rise to dominance in central northern Tanzania of a previously unimportant people, the ancestors of the Dadog, who had taken on their own identity, distinct from that of their proto–Southern Nilotic forebears, not more than a few centuries before. From far northern Tanzania the early Dadog next spread south into the Masai steppe and southwestward into parts of Kondoa, Mbulu, and Singida. But sometime in the first half of the present millennium South Kalenjin people, repeating the earlier Dadog expansion south through Masailand, began the assimilation of the Dadog of those areas, while, since mid-millennium, Dadog territory in Mbulu, Singida, and Kondoa has been whittled away by the steady advance of Bantu and West Rift Cushites. Today the Dadog are once again a relatively unimportant people, restricted to a small country, this time, in the far southwest of their former territories.

DADOG CULTURE

The general outlines of Dadog culture have probably remained little changed since the Dadog first evolved into a separate people. They were and remained, first of all, a cattle-keeping people; they milked and bled their cattle, they kept goats and sheep, and they paid a bridewealth in livestock. But they also

9. See Appendix C.2, which includes Dadog loanwords unique to the Gorowa dialect and thus borrowed subsequent to the separation of Gorowa and Iraqw.

practiced the cultivation of grains, although beyond that their agricultural knowledge was little developed; and they probably had no restriction against hunting, as do some East African peoples. The Dadog settlement pattern probably always has been one of individual family kraals rather than villages. Musical instruments were few among the Dadog, as they were, no doubt, among their proto–Southern Nilotic ancestors. The modern Barabaig, for instance, have only a stiff hide which is beaten in time to singing and dancing. In the way of containers, the Dadog made extensive use of calabashes of several different shapes and sizes. They did use earthen pots, at least for cooking, and they probably found uses also for wooden bowls or platters. Baskets, on the other hand, were probably little known to the Dadog and not used by most Dadog groups.[10]

The continuity of Dadog culture seems paralleled by a more remarkable continuity of "corporate" identity of the Dadog. Through wide areas of northern Tanzania and for a thousand years or more the speakers of Dadog must have considered themselves, and been seen by their neighbors, to be one distinctive people because they have for so long a time been called by forms of the name *Dadog*.

For all the continuities, there have also been significant changes in Dadog culture between earlier times and the present. The presumed original Southern Nilotic cycle of eight age sets dropped out of use among the Dadog at some indeterminate time and was replaced by a system of noncycling generation sets, which itself has now broken down. In agriculture the use of the iron hoe may be a relatively late addition to Dadog farming practices borrowed from some Bantu people.[11] Also, the Dadog in their southward expansion into Tanzania may have been introduced to the cultivation of a grain probably not known to the earlier proto–Southern Nilotic community, namely, bulrush millet. In the way of implements the Dadog appear to have adopted a new kind of shield in place of the older oblong shield of proto–Southern Nilotic times; and they may have added a large type of wooden spoon (Swahili *mwiko*) to their cooking utensils.

10. The general maintenance of these traits is assumed because they occur in modern Dadog culture and appear also to have been traits of the proto–Southern Nilotic ancestors of the Dadog. The ideas put forth below about new developments in Dadog culture during the periods of Dadog history derive also from comparison of recent Dadog culture and reconstructed ancient Southern Nilotic culture. For a discussion of proto–Southern Nilotic culture see Chapter 4.

11. The Dadog word for "hoe" seems to be from Bantu. See Appendix E.6.

While the general picture of the Dadog as primarily herders living in scattered homesteads probably held true for most early Dadog peoples, there may well have been local differences in economy. The variety of territory and of neighboring cultures encountered by the Dadog would certainly enhance the possibility of local Dadog variation in patterns of subsistence. The Dadog of the drier portions of the Masai steppe, for instance, could have had to give up cultivation because of the low rainfall and turn entirely to herding. Another possibility worth investigation is that some Dadog groups in far northern Tanzania might have lived in villages and engaged in irrigation agriculture, as do the Sonjo there today. Some sort of close relations between the early Sonjo and Dadog are required in any case by the kinds of Dadog loanwords in Sonjo, and perhaps the participation of both Sonjo and some of the Dadog in the same kind of subsistence activities in the same general region would provide the conditions for such close relations.

CHAPTER 8

The Kalenjin and Their Neighbors

THE PROTO-KALENJIN COMMUNITY

By the beginning of the present millennium proto-Kalenjin peoples lived somewhere in a belt of country running southwest from Mount Elgon to the rift valley. The closely related Kitoki Southern Nilotes lived to their west; the Kenya-Kadam Southern Nilotes may still have lived in the countries bordering them on the north. Between the Kalenjin and Lake Victoria were scattered various Bantu-speaking peoples: the ancestors in language of the Gusii, Kwaya, and others in parts of the regions their descendants inhabit today; the ancestral Luhyia-Gishu groups already in areas north of the Kavirondo Gulf, where they had important contacts with Kitoki Southern Nilotes; and the southeast Elgon Bantu in parts of the country on and below the southeast slopes of Mount Elgon (see Map 8).

The proto-Kalenjin economy was probably little different from recent economies of Kalenjin peoples. The older Southern Nilotic grain-agriculture emphasis was carried over into Kalenjin times. Very likely the proto-Kalenjin still made no important use of the iron hoe, but they brewed both honey and millet beer, as well as palm wine in some areas. They knew of yams, it is clear, but apparently did not cultivate sweet potatoes till much later. Knowledge of this root crop seems generally to have come later to Kalenjin peoples from their neighbors to the west.[1] They may have cultivated bananas; they should at least have known of bananas through their contacts with banana-cultivating Bantu west of them. But there are no reconstructible proto-Kalenjin words dealing with bananas or banana cultivation. It would seem safe to say that the fruit had little or no part in the proto-Kalenjin diet.[2]

Livestock-raising was the other important economic activity of the proto-Kalenjin. They both bled and milked their cattle. When they butchered their cattle, they considered very fatty pieces of meat a special delicacy; meat they did not eat right away they preserved by drying. They had cowbells of some kind. Along with sheep and goats, the proto-Kalenjin also kept donkeys; but

1. Nandian *ropuon*, "sweet potato," comes from Luo, for example.
2. For the vocabulary of proto-Kalenjin culture and economy see Appendix A.5.

while they knew of domestic fowl, chickens were probably of as little importance as they are today among Kalenjin peoples. Interestingly enough, they were acquainted with camels, but this knowledge may have come to them only indirectly from their northern neighbors.[3]

For containers the proto-Kalenjin made extensive use of wood, calabashes, and hides. Wood was fashioned into bowls and beehives and perhaps other containers.[4] The proto-Kalenjin had also as many as three kinds of sacks, since three different words for "sacks" can be reconstructed. In addition, they had the sacklike container for collecting honey still widely used today, quivers for arrows, and scabbards for swords. They also utilized hollowed-out horns for cupping and probably drinking, but they had little use for baskets. Cooking they did in earthen pots, but calabashes were used for carrying and storing milk and beer and perhaps water. Calabash preparation and use must have been of special importance for the proto-Kalenjin. Proto-Kalenjin words for "calabash plant," "green calabash seeds," "dried calabash seeds," for several kinds and shapes of calabashes, and for a stick for cleaning calabashes can all be reconstructed.

As for proto-Kalenjin society, it too must have been little different from many of the recent Kalenjin societies. The basic factor in social relations and the political structure of the society was an age-set system with fixed names working in a recurring cycle. In order, the age sets were (1) $s\mathit{o}$:we, (2) *$koronkoro$, (3) *$k\mathit{i}pk\mathit{o}$:$\mathit{i}m\epsilon t$, (4) *$kaple$:la:c, (5) *$kimnyikeu$, (6) *$ny\mathit{o}$:nki, (7) *$maina$, (8) *cu:ma. A man belonged to an age set for life but advanced from one age grade to another along with the rest of the members of his age set. After circumcision and a brief period of seclusion with his age mates, usually when he was somewhere in his teens, he became a member of the warrior age grade. About fifteen years later, when the next age set younger than his became warriors, he and his age mates entered the elder grade, in which they were to remain for the rest of their lives. Litigation and political decision-making were functions of the local assembly, which consisted of all the men of a particular locality who belonged to the elder age grade.[5]

3. The ultimate source of the proto-Kalenjin word for "camel," *$t\mathit{o}m(p)\epsilon s$, seems to be the root of proto–West Rift *$tsamas$, "giraffe." Perhaps Southern Cushites were in a position to learn about camels first, and then passed that information on to the Kalenjin.

4. Possibly a storage barrel; see entry *to:kei in Appendix A.5.

5. The interpretation of the shape of the society described by the reconstructible proto-Kalenjin vocabulary follows from the meanings of the words in the context of recent Kalenjin societies. For descriptions of modern Kalenjin societies see, for example, G. W. B. Huntingford, *The Nandi of Kenya* (London: Routledge & Kegan Paul, 1953), and *The Southern Nilo-Hamites* (London: International African Institute, 1953).

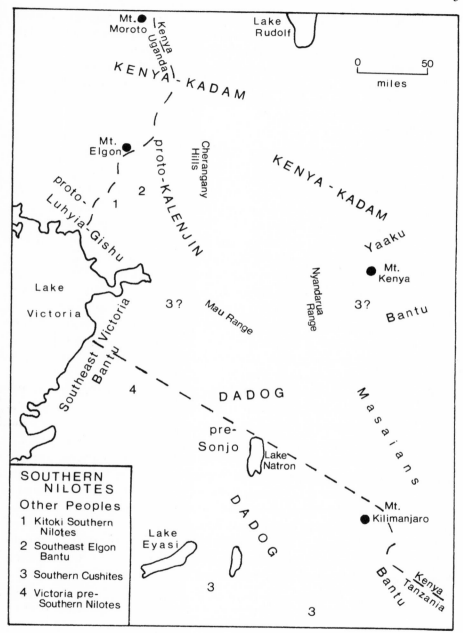

MAP 8. The Proto-Kalenjin and Their Neighbors, ca. 1000 A.D.

Proto-Kalenjin musical instruments were few. They used an animal horn, probably that of the greater kudu, as an instrument, and they also had a lyre. On the other hand, they very probably did not have drums.[6]

While the proto-Kalenjin made their clothing of animal hides, they nevertheless also appear to have known of cloth. For adornment they utilized different kinds of copper rings and bracelets along with beads, leglets of bells, and some ivory.

THE BREAKUP OF THE PROTO-KALENJIN COMMUNITY

The early centuries of the present millennium were marked by the gradual expansion of the Kalenjin peoples and the gradual dialect differentiation which produced the major dialect divisions within Kalenjin that persist today. To the west, on the slopes of Mount Elgon, the common ancestors of the modern Elgon Kalenjin—the Kony, Sabiny, and Pok—began to take on a separate identity. Around the Cheranganys and neighboring parts of the Uasin Gishu plains the ancestors of the Pokot probably lived, while in parts of the southern Uasin Gishu plateau and bordering areas the proto-Nandian dialect was spoken. To the southeast, into the rift valley and surrounding country, other Kalenjin peoples spread early in this millennium. Besides the South Kalenjin, whose only descendants today are the Akie Dorobo of south Masailand, these included peoples speaking dialects ancestral to the Kalenjin Dorobo (East Kalenjin) dialects of Kenya (see Map 9).

The basic evidence for locating the different Kalenjin communities of the first half of the present millennium is the distribution of their descendants today. The Elgon group of peoples, of course, extend around the south and north of Mount Elgon from the east side; the Pokot extend north from the area of the Cheranganys; and the Nandian peoples stretch along the south of the Elgon and Pokot peoples, from the Kipsigis, Nandi, and Terik in the west to the Tuken, Keyo, and Marakwet in the east. The belt of Nandian peoples was presumably continuous across the intervening southern Uasin Gishu plains before it was broken by the Wuasinkishu Masai settlement in the second half of this millennium. The Kenya Dorobo are of course today found to the south and east of the main Nandian-speaking areas, while the remaining South Kalenjin community lives in Tanzania.

6. The evidence on drums is negative, i.e., the lack of a proto-Kalenjin word for drum. But the conclusion is also supported by the general rarity of drums today among the Southern Nilotes.

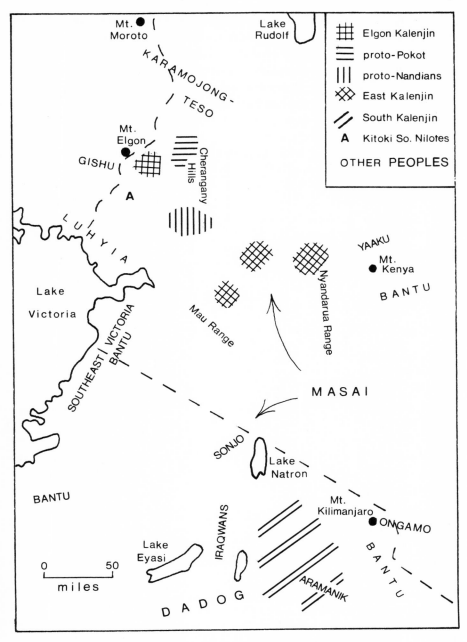

MAP 9.   The Kalenjin, ca. 1400–1500 A.D.

The relative positions assigned the early Kalenjin communities of this millennium are also required by the evidence of interdialect contacts. The ancestral Pokot were in contact on the one hand with the Nandian community, in particular with eastern members of that group, and on the other with the Elgon peoples; while the Elgon community, at least its southern members, were in contact with western Nandian people. These contacts show up in the peculiar word-sharings between Pokot and Elgon dialects, between Pokot and the eastern Nandian dialects, and between Nandi and Kony.[7] The Pokot and Elgon contacts are also evident in their partial sharing of a common sound innovation, the development of central vowels. In the southeast the early interconnections between the peoples speaking the ancestor dialect of one East Kalenjin speech[8] and the South Kalenjin community are attested similarly in peculiar word-sharings between the modern dialects.[9] East Kalenjin in its turn has clear special word-sharings with the Nandian dialects. The separation of these Kalenjin of the southeast from the Elgon Kalenjin of the northwest is conversely clear from their particular lack of any special dialect-sharings.[10]

THE DECLINE OF THE KITOKI SOUTHERN NILOTES

To the immediate west of the Kalenjin the Kitoki Southern Nilotes continued to maintain a separate existence until well into the present millennium. Only gradually were they absorbed by the expanding Luhyia- and Gishu-speaking Bantu. The earliest Bantu word-borrowings from Kitoki Southern Nilotic are common to all the Luhyia-Gishu group:[11] the words were borrowed at a period when the ancestral Luhyia-Gishu were still one people or at most a very closely interrelated group of peoples. But a Kitoki Southern Nilotic dialect may still have been spoken in the Bungoma area as late as Bukusu settlement there, about three centuries ago, because a few words from a

7. E.g., Pokot and the eastern Nandian dialects share a root *kɔ:kɛ:l- for "star," while Nandi and Kony share a different root, *kecɛi-.
8. This is the Kenya Dorobo dialect recorded in G. W. B. Huntingford, "Modern Hunters: Some Account of the Kamelilo-Kapchepkendi Dorobo (Okiek) of Kenya Colony," *Journal of the Royal Anthropological Institute*, LIX (1929), 333–78.
9. E.g., Kamelilo *lano* and Akie *la:nɛ:*, "horn."
10. This separation is also evident from cognate-counting in a basic vocabulary, where Akie and Kamelilo consistently count the lowest rate of sharing with Kony and the highest with Nandian and each other. See Appendix A.1.
11. See Appendix D.9.

Kitoki dialect appear to be unique to Bukusu.[12] Some of the process, then, of Kitoki Southern Nilotic assimilation by the Bantu falls within reach of oral tradition. But not all the aboriginal peoples absorbed in the Luhyia advance were Kitoki Southern Nilotes; in eastern Luhyia country the earlier inhabitants appear instead to have been Kalenjin people, probably Nandian in speech.[13] The Kitoki Southern Nilotes presumably lived more to the central and western parts of Luhyia territory.

Not a great deal can be said about their economy and culture. There is no reason to think it was much different in general outlines from Kalenjin society. Cattle must have been very important: Bukusu borrows its words for "steer" and "to bleed cattle" from Kitoki Southern Nilotic, while the common Luhyia-Gishu words for "to castrate" and "to keep livestock" also come from it. If the Bukusu cycle of eight age-set names can be attributed to the Kitoki Southern Nilotes, then they had also the Southern Nilotic age organization.[14] Possibly they put greater emphasis on banana and root-crop cultivation than the Kalenjin, but this cannot presently be determined.

EARLY NORTHERN KALENJIN PEOPLES

To the north the Kalenjin may still have had the Kenya-Kadam people as neighbors in the first centuries of this millennium. By mid-millennium, however, their Kenya-Kadam neighbors had certainly disappeared there before the expansion of Karamojong-Teso peoples. This expansion was not one of those recorded in the traditions of modern Karamojong-Teso peoples; rather it was an earlier expansion of a community whose presence is recorded only in its effect on the vocabulary and culture of the Pokot. Numerous loanwords from a Karamojong-Teso–related dialect occur throughout the cultural vocabulary of both Pokot dialects.[15] That the words are found everywhere in Pokot speech shows that the loanword period they represent preceded the expansion of the Pokot and the development of the eastern and western Pokot dialects.[16] A very few centuries must be allowed for Pokot expansion over their present territory and to explain the development of slight dialect differences. Further time must be allowed for the type of

12. See Appendix D.11.
13. See Appendix D.10.
14. See Appendix D.11.
15. See Appendix G.1.
16. For dialect classification see A. N. Tucker and M. A. Bryan, "Noun Classification in Kalenjin: Päkot," *African Language Studies*, III (1962).

contact between the Pokot and the Karamojong-Teso group that would account for the thorough penetration of Pokot speech by loanwords from the language of these Karamojong-Teso–speaking neighbors. Thus the beginning of contacts between the two peoples could hardly be put later than mid-millennium.

The Karamojong-Teso people who settled to the north of the early Pokot had an extraordinarily strong effect not only on vocabulary but on Pokot culture. Alone among the Kalenjin, the Pokot assimilate in dress and equipment to the Karamojong-Teso peoples.[17] For instance, they use the long narrow Karamojong type of shield, wear lip plugs, and dress their hair in the style of their northern neighbors. Among some of the northern Pokot even the Southern Nilotic cycling age-set system has been lost. The continuing presence of Karamojong-Teso peoples as neighbors of the Pokot has meant that cultural assimilation has gone on into recent times, so not all the traits the Pokot have borrowed from the Karamojong-Teso were adopted during the original contact period.

While Pokot contacts were beginning with their Karamojong-Teso neighbors, the Elgon peoples were expanding about Mount Elgon. Very little can as yet be said from the linguistic evidence about the course of those expansions. The Kony certainly came into contact with a Bantu-speaking people, the descendants apparently of the Bantu who already lived in the country southeast from Mount Elgon in proto-Kalenjin times or earlier.[18] These people have now disappeared and so must be assumed to have been absorbed by their Elgon-speaking successors. Whether other Elgon peoples had a part in the contacts with this Bantu community and whether they encountered still other peoples in their separate histories can be determined once better knowledge of their cultural vocabularies has been obtained.

THE NANDIAN PEOPLES

Further south the proto-Nandian community may still have been in contact with remaining Southern Cushitic groups, descendants of the Southern Cushites who affected the histories of both the late pre–Southern Nilotes and the immediate ancestors of the Kalenjin. Some apparent Southern Cushitic loanwords appear only in Nandian, but in insufficient numbers to demonstrate

17. Cf. Huntingford, *The Southern Nilo-Hamites,* pp. 15, 16.
18 See Appendixes E.2 and E.3.

conclusively that they are late Southern Cushitic loans rather than older Southern Cushitic loanwords in proto-Kalenjin which happened to survive only in Nandian.[19]

The most important external contacts for the Nandian peoples in the centuries before and around mid-millennium, though, were with Bantu-speaking peoples to their west. Specifically, these contacts seem to have been with people speaking a dialect close to Gusii. This conclusion is dictated by the particular words borrowed and by the phonology of the words. For instance, the root of Nandian *mokombe, "hoe," occurs only in Gusii and very closely related Kuria among East Victoria Bantu languages; moreover, the Nandian borrowing has o for Bantu *u and e for Bantu *i, as do Gusii and Kuria.[20] Of the Bantu loanwords peculiar to Nandian, several are agricultural in reference, but there are others that are not specifically agricultural. The agricultural words probably point up a continuing significance of the Bantu to the west for agricultural innovation among the Kalenjin. The loanword set requires, however, no more explanation than long-continued contact of neighboring peoples.

The Bantu loanword set in Nandian is matched on the Bantu side by Kalenjin loanword sets in Gusii and in eastern Luhyia dialects. Some of these seem specifically Nandian in source, as, for instance, in Idakho and in Gusii.[21] Nandian-speaking populations, then, appear formerly to have been spread in the Kavirondo Gulf area somewhat west of their present territories. But since the gradual breakup of proto-Nandian probably dates to near mid-millennium, Nandian expansion into parts of Nyanza Province was often no earlier than countervaling Bantu expansion. In the resulting competition for land the Bantu-speakers usually won out and absorbed the Nandians, but not without effect on their vocabularies.[22]

19. The Southern Cushitic loanword set in Gusii seems limited to that language. If so, the contacts it indicates would have to be set in relatively recent times and would therefore require a Southern Cushitic population in parts of the western highlands just as recently. The primary question is whether the words appear in Kuria, which is easily interintelligible with Gusii. If not, Southern Cushites had to have lasted well into the present millennium. But knowledge of Kuria is as yet inadequate on this point.

20. See Appendix E.4. The same word for "hoe" occurs elsewhere in Bantu as omukumbi in Ganda and mukumbi in Chaga.

21. See Appendixes D.10 and D.14.

22. For Luhyia traditions of these interactions see G. S. Were, *A History of the Abaluyia of Western Kenya* (Nairobi: East African Publishing House, 1967).

CHAPTER 9

Kalenjin Peoples along the Rift Valley

THE EAST KALENJIN

The steady and rather slow differentiation of the proto-Kalenjin in the western highlands into a number of successor communities was paralleled by a territorially much larger and more rapid expansion of Kalenjin through the rift-valley countries. The remaining East and South Kalenjin speakers are the descendants in language of these early rift-valley Kalenjin (see Map 9).

The early East Kalenjin, who lived through the rift areas east of the proto-Nandian community during the first half of this millennium, may have begun as a single people speaking one dialect of proto-Kalenjin, or they may have belonged from the first to two or more independent groups. The dialects of their linguistic descendants, the Kalenjin-speaking Dorobo of Kenya, are as yet too little known for this question to be satisfactorily answered. At the least, the Kamelilo, Eldama Ravine, and Ndoro dialects, for which some words have been collected,[1] have been separated for some centuries, for they have notable differences in inherited Kalenjin vocabulary and different loan-word histories.[2]

The Kamelilo dialect is well enough known for some statement to be made about the history of its speakers. Contacts between the East Kalenjin and the Sonjo seem reflected in a small set of words peculiar to the Kamelilo dialect and Sonjo.[3] Presumably either Sonjo country formerly extended farther north or the territory of some of the East Kalenjin extended farther south. Masai dominance in recent centuries accounts for numerous loanwords in Kamelilo, but there are also a number of words which appear Masai in origin by reason of containing fossil Masai prefixes, but which are not used in modern Masai. Apparently the recent Masai of the rift-valley country were preceded by other Masai-speaking peoples, related in language but speaking a different dialect.[4]

1. G. W. B. Huntingford, "Modern Hunters: Some Account of the Kamelilo-Kapchep-kendi Dorobo (Okiek) of Kenya Colony," *Journal of the Royal Anthropological Institute,* LIX (1929), and C. W Hobley, "Further Notes on the El Dorobo or Oggiek," *Man,* V (1905), 21.
2. See Appendix A.6.
3. See Appendix B.5.
4. See Appendix G.2.

Attributable to this stratum are such basic words as "bird" and "blood." The earlier Masai-speakers must have held every bit as dominant a position in the rift-valley areas as the later Masai.

The result of this history of long Masai domination has been the restriction of East Kalenjin speech to isolated hunter-gatherer groups scattered through country of Masai-speaking people. Though the original East Kalenjin were surely farmers or at least herders, no food-producing communities have remained among their linguistic descendants. The reorganization of society occasioned by Masai settlement led to assimilation of East Kalenjin pastoralists by Masai pastoralists but left separate the Dorobo, with their radically different economy. The question for future investigation is how, in the first place, so many Dorobo bands came to speak East Kalenjin dialects if even the subsequent long, dominant Masai presence was insufficient to influence them to adopt Masai in place of Kalenjin.

THE EARLY SOUTH KALENJIN COMMUNITY

South Kalenjin, today like East Kalenjin dialects in being spoken only by hunter-gatherers, was once the most widely spoken Kalenjin dialect. Its earliest speakers, food-producers in economy, evolved as a separate group on the far southeast of the proto-Kalenjin country. At first neighbors of the East Kalenjin in south central Kenya, they began to spread southward into Tanzania probably well before the middle of the present millennium. Consideration of the time requirements of population shifts suggests this dating. The Masai, who succeeded the South Kalenjin in Masailand, were already in the far south of that region by the 1700's[5] and may have been preceded there by an earlier Masai-speaking people.[6] Several generations each would have to be counted back before the eighteenth century to allow time for the Masai expansions. Before that, several more generations had to have passed to account for South Kalenjin occupation of the whole length of Masailand, and several more generations after the South Kalenjin had obtained dominance in the far south to account for Dorobo adoption of the speech of the newcomers. Even if only one Masai-speaking people ever lived in Masailand, the South Kalenjin expansion could hardly have begun later than mid-millennium.

5. Personal communication from Alan Jacobs.
6. See below, pp. 75, 76.

As the South Kalenjin populations moved southward, they must have assimilated the Dadog-speakers who had preceded them in large parts of northern and central, if not southern, Masailand.[7] There are a very few words peculiar to Dadog and Akie which may evidence this contact and assimilation.[8]

The South Kalenjin also came into contact with Southern Cushites and Bantu. The Southern Cushites spoke a language related especially closely to Aramanik, the language of the hunting people who today live among the Masai in central Masailand.[9] The Bantu spoke a dialect close to modern Zigula and neighboring dialects of eastern Tanzania.[10] The location of these related peoples today shows that the earlier South Kalenjin contacts with their congeners should be sited nearby, that is, in central and southern Masailand. The Bantu loanwords in Akie indicate a moderately important contact period for the Kalenjin community. The words include those, for instance, for "egg," "bushpig," and "flour." Perhaps Bantu peoples once lived farther into South Masailand than today, because the Southern Cushites from whom the South Kalenjin borrowed words had themselves had contacts with the same Bantu.[11] The Southern Cushitic loanwords in Akie could indicate for south Masailand an earlier Southern Cushitic food-producing community, large enough by reason of their type of economy to leave the evidence of their presence in South Kalenjin vocabulary. Or the loanwords might only identify the language spoken by the hunters of south Masailand before they took over the speech of the dominant South Kalenjin around them.

MASAI PEOPLES AND THE SOUTH KALENJIN

At their height the South Kalenjin were spread from the south of Kenya to the south end of Masailand. Today, of course, the South Kalenjin are restricted to the area of south Masailand; but for quite a while at some earlier period they exerted the dominant influence on Masai history, a fact which necessitates their presence in considerable numbers in areas farther north, where the Masai were then living. This influence shows up clearly in a

7. See above, Chapter 7.
8. See Appendix H.3.
9. See Appendix B.7.
10. See Appendix E.5.
11. In Akie the Southern Cushitic loanword *pango:ku:*, "cave," comes from a still earlier eastern Tanzania Bantu root *-pango*.

heavy general set of South Kalenjin loanwords in Masai. That these Masai words are South Kalenjin in origin is evident in their representation of Kalenjin *ɔ and *ɔː as a, *-yɔː(n) as *-yian, and *wɔː(n) as -uan, all characteristic features of South Kalenjin.[12] The South Kalenjin loans in Masai cover much of the vocabulary except for cattle nomenclature, where they are rare. The strong South Kalenjin influence on vocabulary was probably matched by South Kalenjin influence on Masai cultural development, but such effects as this influence had on Masai practices cannot be clearly distinguished from those arising out of the Masaian–Southern Nilotic contacts which began in the first millennium.

The early South Kalenjin should be viewed as a cattle-keeping people. The mobility this economy gave them may have been a factor in their settlement through the vast Masailand areas of Tanzania. While the South Kalenjin may have emphasized livestock-keeping, cultivation, among at least the more southerly of them, may have had very little significance indeed. The Akie language retains much of the livestock vocabulary it inherited from proto-Kalenjin, but its cultivation vocabulary is largely made up of loanwords, most from a Masai-related dialect but some from an eastern Tanzania Bantu dialect.[13] The Masai-related dialect provides, in particular, important words of the grain-cultivation vocabulary, including the names for "bulrush millet," "sorghum," "porridge," and "gruel."

The loanword set that these words belong to[14] is of great interest because it does not appear to be attributable on linguistic grounds to a recent Masai source, a conclusion in keeping with the culture implications of the loanword set. The Masai-speaking peoples who were knowledgeable in grain agriculture to the extent of so influencing the Akie agricultural vocabulary would hardly seem identifiable with the modern pastoral Masai, who eschew all cultivation. These Masai-speaking agriculturists may have entered southern Masailand after the South Kalenjin, or they may have interacted with the South Kalenjin earlier in their history and farther north, in southern Kenya or northern Tanzania. The second solution requires the least complicated history; and, as loanwords in Kamelilo Dorobo indicate, there were other such Masai-speakers, with a dialect different from modern Masai, in Kenya

12. See Appendix F.3.
13. See Appendixes E.5. and G.3.
14. See Appendix G.3.

earlier in this millennium.[15] But, on the other hand, there are suggestions in Masai tradition of other Masai-speaking peoples preceding them in Masailand,[16] while today Masai-speaking Baraguyu, who do make use of grains and vegetable foods, live scattered through the areas bordering on southern Masailand. So perhaps setting up two Masaian expansions across Masailand is the better solution after all. Better knowledge of Sonjo and especially Aramanik and Baraguyu vocabularies should help greatly in clarifying this problem.

But whatever the details of Masai expansion, probably already by 1600 the extent of South Kalenjin–speaking territory had greatly decreased before the advance of Masai peoples. Today, of course, only the few hundred Akie of far southern Masailand remain of the once widespread and numerous South Kalenjin.

OTHER POSSIBLE KALENJIN IN TANZANIA

Yet another Kalenjin people may have spread rather far south into Masailand. The evidence consists of Kalenjin loanwords in Aramanik. Some of these show the characteristic South Kalenjin change of Kalenjin *ɔ to *a, but others do not; and none have the characteristic South Kalenjin -yan noun suffix. Rather they show -yo, the corresponding suffix in the Nandian and East subgroups of Kalenjin. An example is Aramanik olgoiatiki, "Zauberer," from a Kalenjin source *ɔːrkɔːiyɔ(t)-,[17] where the corresponding Akie stem is aːrkaːyaːn-. The particular linguistic connections of these Kalenjin, then, could well have been with the East Kalenjin or the Nandian. The interesting problem will be to fit this proposed second Kalenjin people into the crowded history of the Masai steppe in the second millennium A.D.—to determine what their linguistic connections were and whether their expansion preceded or followed South

15. Cf. also a couple of curious words in Sonjo: elemur, "brown (cow)," and elepusien, "bluish-gray (cow)." The stems -mur and -pusien are certainly Kalenjin; cf. proto-Kalenjin *mur and *pusie(n). But is the initial ele- from the Masai ol- singular and il- plural noun prefixes? If so, the words come through a dialect different from the modern Masai dialect, one which in turn borrowed the words from Kalenjin, because ele- would require an original prefix el- with a different vowel from the one in modern Masai forms.

16. Personal communication from Alan Jacobs.

17. The final -iki of the Aramanik form is a noun suffix; the final -t of the suggested Kalenjin source would be the Southern Nilotic *t suffix forming the secondary singular form of nouns. In Nandi the same word in its primary form is orkoiyo, in its secondary form orkoiyot. See Appendix C.3.

Kalenjin expansion.[18] Better knowledge of Aramanik vocabulary may provide the key.

18. Still another interesting possibility is that this supposed second Kalenjin people simply spoke a very early form of South Kalenjin, in which Kal *ɔ had not yet become *a*.

CHAPTER 10

The Southern Nilotes in East African History

THE EARLY AND MIDDLE PRE–SOUTHERN NILOTIC PERIODS

The events of Southern Nilotic history before 1600 were played out against a shifting East African backdrop. The earliest Southern Nilotes in south and central Kenya encountered Southern Cushites and aboriginal hunting-gathering peoples. But in succeeding eras Bantu expansion engulfed great areas of East Africa, eclipsing the Southern Cushites almost everywhere. The Southern Nilotes did not escape the effects of this new population pressure. Yet their contacts with remaining Southern Cushites continued to be important long after their first meeting with Bantu immigrants, while, since those first Bantu contacts, the Masaian and Karamojong-Teso peoples, through their expansions across large areas of Kenya, Uganda, and Tanzania, have come to affect the course of Southern Nilotic history more than either the Bantu or the Southern Cushites.

The prelude to Southern Nilotic entrance into these events had its setting farther north. In the earliest era of Southern Nilotic history, the early and middle pre–Southern Nilotic periods, Southern Nilotes probably lived only on the northern periphery of East Africa, where their most significant contacts were with other Nilotes and with the ancestors of the present-day non-Nilotic peoples of far northern East Africa and the adjoining Sudan plains and Ethiopia. In these contacts the early Southern Nilotes would have been participants in a possible culture area characterized by age-set systems, the practice of bleeding cattle, and high value put on cattle. Defined by these traits, the culture area would have centered on the Nilotes of the country between the Nile and the Lake Rudolf area but would have extended east to the southeastern Ethiopian highlands to include the ancestors of the Eastern Cushites. The Eastern Cushites, in the guise of "Hamites," have often been considered as innovators in these cultural developments, but such a role seems hardly likely in view of their location on the far fringe of this proposed culture area. The role better fits the more centrally located Nilotes.

By middle pre–Southern Nilotic times the Southern Nilotes had clearly come to belong with the Eastern Cushites to a more limited and sharply defined culture area. In this smaller culture area the Eastern Cushites did hold a decisively dominant position. Characteristic traits deriving from this period included cycling age-set systems, circumcision, clitoridectomy, and a prohibition against eating fish. The last three items are certainly Cushitic in origin and reflect the great Eastern Cushitic dominance that is evidenced also in loanwords in Southern Nilotic vocabulary. The similarities in Southern Nilotic and Eastern Cushitic age organizations may derive from the same era of Cushitic preeminence or may have developed in the early stages of the evolving special contacts between the Southern Nilotes and Eastern Cushites before the balance began to tip in favor of the Cushites.

The rise of the Eastern Cushites at the expense of the Southern Nilotes need not have required any sudden disruption of previous trends. The early pre–Southern Nilotes and the ancestors of the Eastern Cushites were probably neighbors or near neighbors, and even small and gradual changes in population, aspirations, or attitudes toward each other might have been enough to shift the balance of opportunity from one to the other.

THE SOUTHERN NILOTIC ENTRANCE INTO EAST AFRICA PROPER

While the predicament of the middle pre–Southern Nilotes may well have evolved gradually out of the situation of early pre–Southern Nilotic times, the expansion of their descendants, the late pre–Southern Nilotes, into the heart of East Africa was an abrupt change, not necessarily in location—they may after all have expanded south gradually over a number of generations—but in the direction of their history. They began the period as a people, not numerous, who had become increasingly "Cushitized" and probably, like other peoples in similar situations today, in imminent danger of losing their language and their identity as a separate people. They ended the period as a group of relatively numerous peoples in control of large areas of southern and central Kenya and northern Tanzania. Their movement into those countries had given them new options, and the momentum of their expansion enabled them to take up the options.

The late pre–Southern Nilotes were not the first cultivators and herders in southern and central Kenya. They were certainly preceded by the Southern Cushites, from some of whose languages they borrowed words. Hunter-gatherers were also a significant element in the East African population of the late pre–Southern Nilotic period. That there should have been a proto–

Southern Nilotic word which meant simply "hunting-gathering people" suggests that food-gathering was a widely practiced and, in Southern Nilotic eyes at least, distinctive category of economic activity. Perhaps even the conception of the hunter-gatherer as belonging to another class of people was a distinction introduced by Southern Nilotes. There does not *seem*, at least, to be any comparable Southern Cushitic word.

The late pre–Southern Nilotes, then, entered East Africa as competitors of the Southern Cushites for possession of suitable pasture and cultivable land. They entered a land by no means entirely occupied by people of food-producing economy, but rather from the first they coexisted with hunter-gatherers even as they competed with the herders and cultivators. At the beginning of Christian times there were already several pre–Southern Nilotic peoples scattered through central and southern Kenya, among them the immediate ancestors of the proto–Southern Nilotes. How much earlier than the Christian era the Southern Nilotic expansion into that region began cannot yet be determined, but by the start of the first millennium A.D. the forefront of the Southern Nilotic advance had already carried as far as Tanzania.

THE BANTU AND THE RISE OF THE PROTO–SOUTHERN NILOTES

There, along the Tanzania-Kenya border, the expansion of the late pre–Southern Nilotes came up against the countervailing northward expansion of the Bantu. For a while the pre–Southern Nilotes and Bantu may have divided the territory. The encounter did not immediately bring to an end the expansive tendencies of either people. Along the Lake Victoria shore some of the Bantu carried on their expansion into the country north of the Kavirondo Gulf; southward from the same regions pre–Southern Nilotes pushed into west central Tanzania. But in the nearly two millennia which have passed since the end of the late pre–Southern Nilotic period Bantu-speakers have expanded only a relatively short distance farther into Kenya. They gradually displaced the descendants of the late pre–Southern Nilotes in west central Tanzania, in the southeast Lake Victoria region, and in parts of Kilimanjaro and the eastern highlands of Kenya. But they never did possess the vast plains that stretch along the Kenya-Tanzania borderlands between these areas. For the Southern Nilotes, on the other hand, the encounter with the Bantu coincided with a shift of the impetus of Southern Nilotic expansion from those in the forefront of the southward advance to other Southern Nilotic peoples, in particular the proto–Southern Nilotes and their descendants.

By the middle of the first millennium this new shape of things must have begun to be evident in events in western and central Kenya when out of the breakup of the proto–Southern Nilotic community the ancestors of the Dadog began to spread south through the rift-valley country into northern Tanzania, the Kenya-Kadam peoples moved north and westward across the country between Mount Kenya and eastern Uganda, and the ancestors of the Kalenjin and the Kitoki Southern Nilotes spread through the western highlands of Kenya as far as Mount Elgon. The Southern Nilotes who initiated these new expansions entered into new patterns of interaction with other East African peoples. The Kalenjin and Kitoki Southern Nilotes remained in active contact with Bantu people to their west, and the Kalenjin continued an earlier trend of expansion, of gradually assimilating the prior Southern Cushitic population of the western highlands. But the Kenya-Kadam peoples pressed north into lands where Teso-Masaian and Tepeth-Nyangiya peoples previously dominated, and the Dadog spread south, first through the country of other Southern Nilotes and eventually into the Masai steppe and the highlands of Mbulu and Kondoa, where previously the dominant peoples had spoken Southern Cushitic languages.

THE GROWING IMPORTANCE OF THE EASTERN NILOTES

Of the greatest effect on the future course of Southern Nilotic history, however, were not these expansions but the breakup of the proto–Teso-Masaian community. The breakup of this Eastern Nilotic–speaking people began only after they had come into contact with northward-spreading descendants of the proto–Southern Nilotes, and it is possible that the resulting Teso-Masaian expansions were in part a reaction to Southern Nilotic pressure. Out of the splitting-up of the community the proto-Masaian peoples spread into parts of central south Kenya, absorbing Southern Nilotic people who preceded them there, while the ancestors of the Karamojong-Teso peoples may have continued for some time to live in much the same country as their proto–Teso-Masaian ancestors. It is these two sets of peoples who account for most of the decline in territory that the Southern Nilotes have suffered since the height of their expansion around the end of the first millennium A.D., when they inhabited large parts of northwestern, western, central, and southern Kenya and adjoining northern Tanzania and smaller parts of eastern Uganda. The Masai, in particular, in the present millennium took over the vast territories they inhabited by the mid-1800's by directly assimilating the previous Southern Nilotic–speaking population; and the Ongamo, whose language also descends from proto-Masaian, contributed to the disappearance of Southern Nilotic peoples from the Kilimanjaro area. Karamojong-Teso expansion, in its turn, brought about the retreat of Southern Nilotic territory in northwestern Kenya and neighboring eastern Uganda.

Although Southern Nilotes on the whole have declined in territory, and no doubt in relative numbers, since the close of the first millennium A.D., the era has been one characterized not by steady decline but by great fluctuation in the importance of the Southern Nilotes. That it was not a period only of decline was due to vigorous population expansion among the Kalenjin peoples. In the Mount Elgon and Kavirondo Gulf area the Kitoki Southern Nilotes on the one hand disappeared in the face of Bantu expansion, but Kalenjin-speaking people on the other expanded their territory at the expense of at least one former important Bantu community. Similarly, in western Kenya north of the western highlands the former Kenya-Kadam peoples have been entirely assimilated, but a portion of their country has been regained in recent centuries by the Pokot. And while the Masai did at their height inhabit the whole rift-valley country of Kenya and Masailand of Tanzania, through much of the area their expansion had been preceded in the same present millennium by very nearly as great an expansion of Kalenjin people.

COMMON THEMES IN SOUTHERN NILOTIC HISTORY

Through these events run several recurrent themes. The most striking, perhaps, consists in the successive expansions of Southern Nilotes out of the region of the western highlands and adjoining rift-valley country of Kenya. The spread of the descendants of the proto–Southern Nilotes in the first millennium A.D. as well as the Kalenjin expansions of the present millennium certainly derive from this region; and since the original Southern Nilotic settlement which opened the late pre–Southern Nilotic period lay somewhere in the same general area, the eventual spread of pre–Southern Nilotes as far south as northern Tanzania must also have emanated from there.

A complementary theme is the role of northern Kenya and of the combined regions of the Kenya rift valley and the Masai plains of Tanzania as the areas

of greatest territorial expansion in the two more recent of these three population movements. In the era of expansion following the proto–Southern
Nilotic period the Kenya-Kadam peoples advanced across the dry north,
while the Dadog pushed southward, through central Tanzania Masailand at
least. In the Kalenjin expansion period the Pokot spread well into the dry
country north of the western highlands, whereas the South Kalenjin spread
south through all of Masailand. In each period Southern Nilotic expansion in
the western highlands covered much less territory and by all appearances was
less rapid.

Another important theme of the past two millennia has been the wide-
ranging competition for territory between the Southern Nilotes and certain of
the Eastern Nilotes. In a majority of the areas where the Southern Nilotes
have settled during this period they have eventually come into conflict with
Karamojong-Teso or Masaian peoples. With Masaian peoples they have
struggled for control of the southern Kenya plains and Masailand; with the
Karamojong-Teso, for dominance in the lower country north of the western
highlands.

In contrast, Southern Nilotic contacts with Bantu have been limited for the
most part to the east shore of Lake Victoria, to country about the eastern
highlands of Kenya, and to Kilimanjaro. A secondary theme in Southern
Nilotic, in particular Kalenjin, contacts with Bantu has been the indebtedness
of the Southern Nilotes to Bantu for innovations in agriculture.

The recurrence of such themes requires more explanation than the chance
confluence of events. The probable determinants are economic: the events
may derive from the effects on migration of different patterns of subsistence.
The basic proposition underlying such an explanation is that people tend to
move where they can continue to live by the methods of subsistence they are
accustomed to and know how to use effectively. Two major patterns of food
production are followed in the parts of East Africa where the Southern Nilotes
live and have lived: (1) herding, along with grain cultivation; (2) cultivation,
with bananas and root crops prominent, along with some herding. Peoples
practicing the first subsistence pattern could live anywhere within the
Southern Nilotic and erstwhile Southern Nilotic regions, whereas peoples
following the second pattern would tend to be restricted to the wetter areas,
namely, the Lake Victoria shore and parts of the western highlands, parts of
the eastern highlands of Kenya, and the slopes of Kilimanjaro. Thus Bantu,
who emphasized the cultivation of root crops and bananas, came into

competition with Southern Nilotes only in those particular areas. But the
Southern Nilotes, as herders and grain cultivators, and the Southern Cushites and Eastern Nilotes, who had similar subsistence practices, have been
able to expand into areas with all kinds of climate and terrain.

A complementary proposition is that the herding and grain-cultivating
economy would generally allow greater population mobility, especially if the
culture strongly emphasized herding. Such an economy requires at least
local mobility because of the continual need to find grazing for the stock, and
as a consequence the material culture of peoples with this economy tends to
consist of lightweight, easily movable items. If a people feel the need or desire
to move, their belongings are easy to pack up and carry; and a major source of
subsistence, their livestock, can move along with them. Thus it becomes
understandable that the areas of repeated and territorially extensive Southern
Nilotic, as well as Eastern Nilotic, expansion should have been the country
north of the western highlands and, above all, the plains of southern Kenya
and adjoining Masailand, regions where population has always been relatively
scanty and subsistence activities, primarily herding, would not greatly have
hindered migration. The slower and more circumscribed population movements in the western highlands and Lake Victoria shore areas probably reflect, on the other hand, the greater orientation of the people toward cultivation
and their lesser need of mobility, because grazing was usually near at hand
by reason of the better rainfall.

A further proposition is that a wetter climate would, in providing better
grazing, producing higher grain yields, and allowing more different crops to
be grown, support a larger population. A more favorable climate could help
to explain why the source of successive Southern Nilotic migrations seems to
have been west and central Kenya. The western highlands and rift-valley
area, as high and relatively well-watered country, could be expected to have
had a much higher population density than drier Masailand and northern
Kenya and, located between the two drier areas, could have served as a
reservoir for Southern Nilotic population expansion.

Recourse to an idea of a population "reservoir" does not require any accom-
panying assumption of overpopulation to explain population movement.
The eventual expansion of people out of a more thickly populated region into
less populated country could be seen as simply the long-run effect of the usual
mutual raiding between adjoining peoples who both graze many cattle. The
people in the drier, less heavily settled country would have fewer neighbors to

summon for help in event of attack, and their neighbors would live farther away and be longer in coming to their assistance. Less well equipped, therefore, to defend themselves from attack, they would tend to suffer more from being raided by people of the nearby, more thickly populated country than those nearby people would suffer from their counterraids. Often over the long run the people of the less densely peopled region would be unable to sustain their position and would have to accommodate to the resulting pressure on their territory, whether by alliance and intermarriage with people from the more heavily populated neighboring region or by retreat from the areas of conflict. In either case, the result would be the advance of influences and people from the more to the less densely settled area.

An especially strong and well-developed military tradition could, as for the Masai, offset or reverse for awhile the usual disadvantage of a people from the more sparsely occupied region. But a society would change over time. New external factors could shift a power balance so delicately dependent on maintenance of traditional attitudes or, if not external pressure, then the internal stresses which arise in any successful society as its members struggle over the distribution of success. In such a manner internecine fighting among the Masai from mid-nineteenth century on deeply threatened their position in central Kenya and might eventually have opened the way to a possible Kalenjin resurgence.

By the 1600's and 1700's, when oral tradition begins among the Southern Nilotes, these patterns of history had left this legacy: the Kalenjin of the western highlands, the Southern Nilotes who lived nearest the older centers of Southern Nilotic settlement, were thriving and growing in numbers. The Dadog and South Kalenjin, who had expanded farthest, were in decline before the spread of other peoples. The Bantu had not gained greatly at the expense of the Southern Nilotes, but the Eastern Nilotes, whose economies were especially well adapted to the great East African plains, which the Southern Nilotes had long and often controlled, had gained a great deal indeed. Given time, control of much of this country might yet again have passed to the more numerous Southern Nilotic–speaking peoples. But between then and now an entirely new factor, the colonial era, diverted the stream of East African history, and the old forces no longer operate.

APPENDIXES

NOTE TO THE APPENDIXES

The first of the following series of appendixes contains nonloanword evidence for Southern Nilotic history; the other six series contain the loanword evidence. Numerous abbreviations and unfamiliar linguistic signs are used in the appendixes; for explanation of these, see the lists below. The criteria for particular loanword determinations are also given in abbreviated form, in the "Source" column in each appendix. The reader should refer to Chapter 2 for explanation of the criteria applied. In a few cases the reason for a loan determination is given as "pattern." This notation means that the loanword shows the same particular feature as other loanwords in a language, the sources of which can be determined on other, firmer evidence.

ABBREVIATIONS OF NAMES OF PEOPLES AND THEIR LANGUAGES

Aram.	Aramanik	Mas	Masaian
B	Bantu	Mas.	Masai
Buk.	Bukusu	Nd	Nandian
Bur.	Burungi	Nil	Nilotic
Cush	Cushitic	pt	proto-
Dah.	Dahalo	Rav.	Ravine Dorobo dialect (East Kalenjin)
Eastn	Eastern		
ECush	Eastern Cushitic	SCush	Southern Cushitic
ENil	Eastern Nilotic	SEVicB	Southeast Victoria Bantu
ERift	East Rift	Sid.	Sidamo
EVicB	East Victoria Bantu	SKal	South Kalenjin
Gor.	Gorowa	SNil	Southern Nilotic
Id.	Idakho	Som.	Somali
Ir	Iraqwan	SW	Southwest
Ir.	Iraqw	Tanz.	Tanzania
Kal	Kalenjin	Tep.	Tepeth
Kam.	Kamelilo	Tind.	Tinderet Dorobo dialect (East Kalenjin)
Kik.	Kikuyu		
KT	Karamojong-Teso	TMas	Teso-Masaian
Log.	Logoli	WRift	West Rift

assimil.	assimilated
C	consonant
caus.	causative
consectv	consecutive
deriv	derivation
diff.	different
dissimil.	dissimilation
distrib	distribution
ext.	extension
init.	initial
interprt.	interpreted
intrusv	intrusive
morphol	morphology
n.	noun
phonol	phonology
pl.	plural
pref.	prefix
sec.	secondary
sing.	singular
specif.	specific
suff.	suffix
ultim.	ultimately
unprodc	unproductive
V	vowel
v.	verb
var.	variety

LINGUISTIC SIGNS AND THEIR APPROXIMATE PRONUNCIATIONS

ə	like *u* in "b*u*t"
ʌ	similar to ə but with a higher tongue position
i	similar to *u* in "j*u*st" used as an adverb in American English
æ	like *a* in "h*a*t"
ɪ	like *i* in "h*i*t"

ɛ	like *e* in "b*e*t"
ʊ	like *oo* in "g*oo*d"
ɔ	like *ou* in "b*ou*ght"
î	super-close high front vowel
û	super-close high back vowel
*l*ʸ	like Castilian Spanish *ll* in *caba*llo, "horse"
β	voiced bilabial fricative (to English speakers it sounds most like *v*)
γ	voiced velar fricative
š	like *sh* in "*sh*ed"
c	like *ch* in "*ch*ur*ch*"
ŋ	like *ng* in "si*ng*"
ʔ	glottal stop
ʕ	like Arabic letter *'ayn*
ḥ	like Arabic *ḥ* in "*Aḥ*mad"

OTHER LINGUISTIC SIGNS

:	indicates long vowel; a macron (ˉ) is used to mark length, however, when a word taken from a published work has been marked that way in the work.
*	marks the reconstructed earlier form of a root or affix.
φ	zero; marks lack of element.
-	A hyphen is used to mark the beginning or end of the stem of a word to which an affix is normally attached in actual speech; it also marks the beginning of a suffix and the end of a prefix.

Appendixes A.1–A.7

Nonloanword Evidence

A.1

Counting of Cognate-sharing between Southern Nilotic Dialects

For cognate-counting among Southern Nilotic dialects and languages the following ninety-item list of basic words was constructed and used: I, you (sing.), we, who, what, all, many, one, two, three, four, five, big, small, long, hot, cold, new, good, dry, black, white, red, green, to eat, to drink, to bite, to see, to hear, to know, to sleep, to die, to kill, to go, to come, to sit, to stand, to give, to say, sun, moon, star, water, rain, cloud, night, smoke, fire, ash, path, mountain, tree, seed, leaf, root, bark, fish, bird, dog, louse, person, man, woman, meat, bone, fat, horn, tail, feather, hair, head, ear, eye, nose, mouth, tooth, tongue, (finger)nail, foot, knee, hand, belly, neck, woman's breast, heart, liver, blood, name, stone, animal.

The figures in the following chart represent the percentage of words shared by each pair of dialects out of the ninety words of the list.

NANDI							
89	TUKEN						
90	90	MARAKWET					
78	81	81	POKOT				
75	74	74	72	KONY			
77	74	74	72	69	AKIE		
(73–80)	(70–78)	(70–78)	(69–77)	(64–72)			
*76	*72	*75	*71	*68	*74	KAMELILO	
(*69–*79)	(*65–*75)	(*67–*78)	(*64–*75)	(*62–*72)	(*63–*79)		
50	49	48	47	45	48	*47	DADOG
					(44–51)	(*43–*53)	

For some of the dialects a few entries were inadvertently not collected or were not available in published evidence. In particular, six words are missing from the Akie collection and, from Kamelilo, nine. On the chart showing their cognate-sharing with other Southern Nilotic dialects, the percentage of words shared out of those actually collected is given, along with a percentage range in parentheses. The high figure of the range is the percentage of the list that would be shared if all of those words not collected were cognates, and the low figure represents the percentage if none were cognates. Neither extreme is likely, and probably the real percentage shared would in every case come within a point or two of the percentage listed outside the parentheses.

A second problem arises in interpreting the Kamelilo cognation. The Kamelilo dialect has borrowed so many basic words from Masai that Kamelilo cognate counts with other Southern Nilotic dialects have been distorted. At least eight or nine of the basic words are Masaian loans. If the older Kalenjin words had not been replaced by these loanwords, the normal expectation from the rates of cognate-sharing among other Kalenjin dialects would have been for about 70–80 per cent of the words still to have been shared with each of the other Kalenjin dialects; that is, $9 \times .70$ to $9 \times .80$, or 6 to 7 words. Thus, what has been given for each Kamelilo entry is a corrected percentage, marked by an asterisk (*). The actual percentage of cognates shared in the ninety-word basic list is in each instance six less than the corrected figure.

A.2

Proto-Nilotic Herding Vocabulary

	Southern Nilotic Attestation	Eastern Nilotic Attestation	Western Nilotic Attestation
Cow	ptSNil *tany	ptENil *-kɪtɛŋ	ptLuo *dhiaŋ, etc.
Goat	ptSNil *no "goats"	ptENil *-kine	
To herd	ptSNil *yaqw-	ptENil *-yok-	
Immature cow	ptSNil *mɔːi "calf" (preSNil *mɔːri)		Dinka mɪɔr "steer"
Udder	Dadog gaːŋoːrjeːd (stem -ŋor-)	Cf. Ongamo nahɪŋɔlɪɔ (stem -ŋɔl-)	Luo nyar, etc.

Less Likely Possible Cognates

He-goat	Dadog qwaraiːd (< *qoroi-)	ptENil *-oro	
Sheep	ptSNil *keːciːr	ptENil *-ker	

A.3

Pre- and Proto–Southern Nilotic Culture Vocabulary

Item or Practice	Late preSNil Reconstruction	ptSNil Reconstruction	Basis of Reconstruction
To herd	*yaqw-	*yaqw-	ptSNil: attested in Dadog, Kal; preSNil: of earlier ptNil origin (see A.2)
Cow	*tany	*tany	See "To herd"
Male bovine	*e:ri	*(y)e:i	ptSNil: attested in Dadog, Kal; preSNil: loss of original r (see Chap. 3)
Bull		*kiru:k	ptSNil: attested in Dadog, Kal
Calf	*mɔ:ri	*mɔ:i	See "Male bovine"
Barren cow	*so:no	*so:no	ptSNil: attested in Dadog, Kal; preSNil: in Victoria SNil loanword set (see D.1)
Cowhide		*mu:i	See "Bull"
Cow's hump	*riu:k	*yu:k	See "Male bovine"
Dewlap		*takol	See "Bull"
Hoof		*pu:tul	See "Bull"
Udder	*koŋo:r-	*koŋo:r-	See "To herd"
Milk	*a:n-	*a:n-	ptSNil: because already preSNil; preSNil: borrowed from ECush in middle preSNil era
Arrow for bleeding cattle		*lʸɔ:(ŋ)-	See "Bull"

Item or Practice	Late preSNil Reconstruction	ptSNil Reconstruction	Basis of Reconstruction
Goat	*mbo:ri	*mbo:i	ptSNil: because already in preSNil; preSNil: loss of original *r* (see Chap. 3)
Goats	*no-	*no-	See "To herd"
He-goat	*qoroi-	*qoroi-	ptSNil: because already in preSNil; preSNil: in Victoria SNil loanword sets (see D.1–D.4)
Young she-goat	*supe:n	*supe:n	See "Milk"
Kid	*wa:r-	*wa:r-	See "Milk"
Sheep		*ke:ci:r	See "Bull"
Donkey	*tike:ri	*tike:i	See "Goat"
Chicken		*inqoq-	See "Bull"
White		*lʸe:lʸ-	See "Bull"
Black	*tu:i-	*tu:i-	See "To herd"
Green		*nyalʸɪ:lʸ- or *nyalɪ:lʸ-	See "Bull"
Red	*piri:r-	*piri:r-	See "He-goat"
Brown, dark brown	*o:mo	*o:mo	ptSNil: attested in Dadog, Kal; preSNil: loanword in Kikuyu (D.6)
Tawny, light brown		*mur-	See "Bull"
Bluish-gray		*pu:sie:n-	See "Bull"
Multicolored		*sa:mu-	See "Bull"
Another coloration (gray?)	*a:ru:s	*a:ru:s	See "He-goat"
To cultivate		*par-	See "Bull"
Eleusine; grain (generic)	*pari	*pai-	See "Male bovine"
Sorghum	*mo:so:ŋ	*mo:so:ŋ	See "Milk"

Item or Practice	Late preSNil Reconstruction	ptSNil Reconstruction	Basis of Reconstruction
Honey barrel	*mori:ŋ(k)-	*moi:ŋ(k)-	See "Goat"
Honey container (sack)		*toqol	See "Bull"
Honey beer		*qomen ?	See "Bull"
Beer straw	*sek-	*sek-	See "He-goat"
To hunt		*lʸɔkɔ:t-	See "Bull"
Iron		*ka:rin-	See "Bull"
To forge		*ta:ny-/*tɔ:ny-	See "Bull"
Branding iron	*mece:ri	*mece:i	See "Male bovine"
Spear		*ŋo:t	See "Bull"
Bow		*qo:a:ŋ-	See "Bull"
Arrow		*kɔ:t-	See "Bull"
Heavy handle (as of ax)		*ku:nyu:k	See "Bull"
Needle, awl	*sʌtek	*sʌtek	See "Barren cow"
Whetstone		*lʸitɛ:i	See "Bull"
Oval Kalenjin shield	*lɔ:ŋ-	*lɔ:ŋ-	ptSNil: attested in Dadog, Kal; preSNil: in preSNil loanword set in ptMas (see F.1)
Calabash	*sot-	*sot-	See "He-goat"
Sack		*mɪlʸo(:t)	See "Bull"
Sack		*lʸɔ:r-	See "Bull"
A (wooden?) container		*(y)a:ra:k-	See "Bull"
Pot		*toi(u:t)	See "Bull"
Copper (ring)		*tɛ:r-	See "Bull"
Cowry		*seke:r-	See "Bull"
Piece of cloth or hide		*a:qwɔ	See "Bull"
Sandal	*kue:riɔ	*kue:iyɔ	See "Male bovine"
Scarification		*sorem-/*sɔrem-	See "Bull"

98

Item or Practice	Late preSNil Reconstruction	ptSNil Reconstruction	Basis of Reconstruction
To circumcise	*mʊr- or *mʊraːt-	*mʊr- or *mʊraːt- or mʊraːtaːn-	See "Milk"
To dance at circumcision	*tuːm-	*tuːm-	ptSNil: attested in Dadog, Kal; preSNil: in preSNil loanword set in Kikuyu (see D.6)
Young man	*mur- or *muren	*mur- or *muren	See "He-goat" and "Oval Kalenjin shield"
Boy, youth		*qaːrʌːmaːn	See "Bull"
Uncircumcised person		*soːmiɔ(ːn)	See "Bull"
Married adult	*kɔːrk-	*kɔːrk-	See "Barren cow"
Age-set names	See A.4	See A.4	
Pauper		*panan	See "Bull"
Hunter-gatherer		*(y)aːk-	See "Bull"
Subtribe		*eːm-	See "Bull"

A.4

Southern Nilotic Age-Set Names

PROTO-KALENJIN AGE-SET CYCLE	KURIA, ETC., AGE-SET CYCLE	RECONSTRUCTED preSNil CYCLE	COMMENTS
*sɔ:we	*-saai	*sɔ:e	a for SNil *ɔ is VicSNil characteristic
*koronkoro	*-gorongoro	*koronkoro	g for SNil *k is common VicSNil development
*kɪpkɔ:ɪmɛt	*-nyambureta	Unknown	
*kaple:la:c	*-gini	?*kini	For reasons see Chap. 5; g for SNil *k: see *koronkoro, above
*kimnyekeu	*-gamunyere	Unknown	
*nyɔ:nki	*-nyangi	*nyɔ:nki	a for SNil *ɔ: see *sɔ:we, above
*maina	*-maina	*maina	
*cu:ma	*-cuuma	*cu:ma	

NOTES: The basis of reconstruction is that the Kuria forms, except -nyambureta and -gamunyere, are presumed loanwords from Victoria Southern Nilotic (see D.2). Since Victoria Southern Nilotic split off from the rest of Southern Nilotic in late pre–Southern Nilotic times, the words' use dates at least to that era.

A.5

Proto-Kalenjin Culture Vocabulary

ITEM OR PRACTICE	ptKal RECONSTRUCTION	COMMENTS
Livestock:		
Cow		
Bull		
Calf		
Barren cow		
Cowhide		
Cow's hump		
Dewlap		
Hoof		
Goats		
Young she-goat		
Kid	See A.3	
Sheep		
Chicken		
White		
Black		
Green		
Red		
Brown, dark brown		
Tawny, light brown		
Bluish-gray		
Multicolored		
Steer	*(y)e:i	All reconstructed forms have reflexes in two or more of coordinate subgroups of Kalenjin dialects, and these reflexes differ in shape according to regular patterns of sound correspondence (see discussion in Chap. 2).
Heifer	*ro:r-	
Old cow	*yo:s-	
Cow dung	*sɪkɔ/*sɪko	
Sheep dung	*soro:i	
Sheepskin	*makata	

Item or Practice	ptKal Reconstruction	Comments
Livestock:		
Udder	*mu:ru:nku*	
To herd	*yakw-*	
Herd	*a:ce:i*	
Cattle fold	*pe:i*	
Salt lick	*ŋe:ny/*ŋe:ŋ*	
Cowbell	*twa:l-/*twɔ:l-*	
Milk	*ce*	
To milk	*kei*	
To bleed	*car*	
Bleeding arrow	*lɔ:ŋ*	
To cut up meat	*sa:c*	
Fatty piece of meat	*su:nɛ:t-*	
Dried meat	*sirkon-*	
Goat, sheep	*a:ra-*	
Goat	*ŋɔrɔ:r*	
He-goat	*kwe:i*	
Male sheep (generic)	*makal*	
Ram	*me:nkic*	
Wether	*seti:m*	
Fowl	*inkok-*	
Donkey	*sɪkɪryɔ*	
Camel	*tɔm(p)ɛs*	
Gray	*ɔ:ru:s* or *a:ru:s-*	
Tawny	*tɔ:lɛ:l-*	
Eland-colored	*si:rua*	
Brown-spotted	*-mu:kiɛ:*	
(Zebra-) striped	*marmar*	
Spotted	*lɛ:kɛ*	
Agriculture:		
Eleusine		
Sorghum	}	See A.3
Honey beer		
Beer straw		

ITEM OR PRACTICE	ptKal RECONSTRUCTION	COMMENTS
Agriculture:		
Upper grindstone	See E.1	
Field	*impar*	
To cultivate	*(i)pat*	
To harvest	*kɛs*	
Ear of grain	*mɛtɛt-*	
To winnow	*sɛ:s*	
Mortar	*kɛ:n*	
Flour	*pʊsia*	
Porridge	*kim-*	
Gruel	*mu:ser*	
Beans	*maka:nta*	
Sugar cane	*mo:p-*	
Yam	*a:ka:n-/*ɔ:kɔ:n-*	
Beer (millet)	*ma:iɣua*	
Palm wine	*porok*	
Utensils, implements:		
Pot		
Calabash (generic)		
Spear		
Bow		
Arrow		
Handle	See A.3	
Shield		
Iron		
To forge		
Branding iron		
Cupping horn	*la:l*	
Honey sack	*tokol*	
A kind of sack	*mɪlo:(t)*	
A kind of sack (small?)	*lɔ:l*	
A kind of sack	*sɔ:mpʊr*	
Basket	*kerep*	
Pot (2)	*ter*	

Utensils, Implements:

Potter's clay	*men-	
Calabash plant	*si:la:(n)kwa	
Dry calabash seeds	*tɛntɛr-	
Green calabash seeds	*(l)a:la:k-	
Beer calabash	*lɔ:e	
Kind of calabash	*mu:ko	
Small calabash	*terek-	
Stick for cleaning calabashes	*so:s-	
Large wooden spoon	*mʊka:ŋ(k)-	
Whetstone	*litɛ:i-	
Quiver	*mɔ:t-	
Bowstring	*i:nɔ	
Scabbard with sword	*co:k-	
Hammer	*kiri:s-	
Bellows	*ko:pa:n	
Greater kudu horn as trumpet	*(ɪ)kɔ:nti	
Lyre	*po:ka:n	
A water container?	*so:i-	Original meaning not clear; Pokot reflex means "horn container for washing hands"; Kamelilo reflex means "jar"
A wooden container?	*tɔ:kei	Original meaning not clear; Pokot reflex means "wooden storage barrel"; Tuken reflex means "woven beer cup"

Society:

Subtribe		
Pauper	} See A.3	
Hunter-gatherer		
Uncircumcised girl		

ITEM OR PRACTICE	ptKal RECONSTRUCTION	COMMENTS
Society:		
People of same part of country?	*poror	Original meaning not clear; Nandi reflex means "age regiment"; Akie reflex means "age set"; Pokot reflex means "neighbors, fellow tribesmen"
District	*kɔːr	
Local assembly	*koːkwa	
Counsellor-elder	*kiːrwɔːkiːn	
Elder	*pɔːi-	
Warrior	*muren	
Person without (many?) cattle	*meːi-	Original meaning not clear; Nandi reflex means "agricultural person"; Kamelilo reflex means "Nandi person"; Pokot reflex means "orphan"
Circumcision ceremony	*tuːm-	
To circumcise	*mʊraːtaːn	
Sponsor of initiate	*moter-	
Seclusion hut for initiates	*mɛːncɔː	
Age set	*(i)pin	
To extract incisor teeth	*yot	
Age-set names	See Chap. 8	
Dress:		
Piece of cloth		
Sandal		
Cowry	See A.3	
Copper (ring)		
Scarification		
Cloth	*anka	
Copper neck ring	*taːe	
Ivory arm clamp	*cepos	
Beads	*soːnai-	
Bell leglet	*-kʊrkʊr-	
Ostrich feather	*soːnkoːl	
Belt	*aːnua	

East Kalenjin Relationships

	KAMELILO	RAVINE	NDORO
Animal	*tiony*	*mugurorit*	*painiek*
Forest	*samak*	*koret*	*timta*
Chest	*teget*	*elgoit* (X)	*ngoro*
Giraffe	+ *tiongangejeya*	*soyogel*	*elmaot* (X)
Rain	*rob*	*eldat* (X)	*mbura*
Firewood	*kwendo*	*kwendet*	*kwenek*
Bone	*kowo*	*oloitit* (X)	*kawit*
To come	*icom-un* (X)	*nyon*	*nyon*
Spear	*olmorondoi* (X)	*tenget*	*tenget*
Sword	*wesek*	*wesekta*	*rotwet*
Hartebeest	+ *rogawiet*	*rogoiwet*	*kishirmut*
Baboon	*konokco*	*elkaldas* (X)	*elkaldas* (X)
Sun	*ceptalil*	*ongollo* (X)	*ongollom* (X)
Buffalo	*tieptatui*	*olusuwan* (X)	*olusuwan* (X)

COMMENTS: The Kamelilo words are taken from G. W. B. Huntingford, "Modern Hunters: Some Account of the Kamelilo-Kapchepkendi Dorobo (Okiek) of Kenya Colony," *Journal of the Royal Anthropological Institute*, LIX (1929). The words there are given a consistent phonetic rendering, though not a completely adequate one from a linguistic point of view. But the evidence for Ravine and Ndoro dialects, drawn from C. W. Hobley, "Further Notes on the El Dorobo or Oggiek," *Man*, V (1905), is often corruptly recorded. The Kamelilo words marked with a plus (+) also come from this source. Nevertheless, the evidence seems to fall into certain patterns, allowing the following tentative conclusions:

(*a*) East Kalenjin dialects more likely than not form a distinct subgroup of Kalenjin, because some words seem to be limited to those dialects alone, e.g., "spear," "sword," and "hartebeest."

(*b*) But the linguistic distance between various East Kalenjin dialects must be fairly great, as is indicated by the number of instances in which the three dialects cited all have different words for a particular meaning; note, above, "animal," "forest," "chest," "giraffe," and "rain."

(*c*) Effective separation of the ancestors of the Ndoro and Ravine Dorobo probably came after the beginning of Masaian influence in the rift-valley country during the present millennium because they share a number of loanwords from Masai, e.g., "baboon," "sun," and "buffalo." The ancestors of the Kamelilo would have separated from the common ancestors of the Ravine and Ndoro Dorobo even earlier, because they do not share in the Masai loanwords common to Ravine and Ndoro. The Ndoro dialect was not greatly affected by Masai contacts after its separation from Ravine but came instead under Kikuyu influence; cf. *mbura*, "rain," which is a Kikuyu loanword.

Note that (X) marks Kamelilo, Ndoro, and Ravine words which are loanwords from Masai.

A.7
Diagram of Southern Nilotic Relationships

proto - Nilotes

Western Nilotes

Eastern Nilotes

late pre-Southern Nilotes

other pre-Southern Nilotes

Victoria pre-Southern Nilotes

proto-Southern Nilotes

pre-Kalenjin

Kitoki Southern Nilotes

Kenya-Kadam

DADOG

proto-Kalenjin

South Kalenjin (AKIE)

East Kalenjin

proto-Nandian

Elgon (KONY, etc.)

POKOT

MARAKWET

TUKEN

NANDI, etc.

Dashes indicate languages no longer spoken

107

Appendixes B.1–B.7

Cushitic Loanword Sets

B.1

Eastern Cushitic Loanwords in Southern Nilotic

SOUTHERN NILOTIC	EASTERN CUSHITIC ATTESTATION	SOURCE	COMMENTS
ptSNil *ro:p- "rain"	Galla rōb- "to rain"; Som. roob- "rain"; Saho rob	Cush: distrib	
ptKal *met "head"	Galla matā; Som. madaḥ; Yaaku mɪtɛh	Cush: distrib; phonol (ḥ)	
ptSNil *pata:i- "back"	Som. baḍi "buttock"; Sid. bade "back"	ECush: distrib; phonol (ḍ)	
ptSNil *mi:e "good"	Saho maˤa "good"; cf. Galla miā, Som. maˤaan "sweet"	Cush: distrib; phonol (ˤ)	
ptSNil *tulua "anthill, hill"	Galla tūlu "hill," tūl- "to heap up"; Som. tuul- "to heap"	Cush: distrib; deriv (< ECush v.)	
ptKal *(i)la:l "to watch, to look"	Galla ilāl- "to look at"; Som. ilaali-; Saho ilal- "to look"	Cush: distrib; ?? deriv (< ? Cush *ila "eye")	
Dadog æ:no:g "milk"	Galla anān; Som. ˤaano-; Saho hān	Cush: distrib; phonol (ˤ)	
ptSNil *(y)e:i (preSNil *e:ri) "male bovine"	Baiso are; Arbore ar, Yaaku ɛrdɪ "bull"	ECush: distrib	preSNil *r
ptKal *supe:n (preSNil *supe:n) "young ewe"	Som. sabeen-	?	
ptKal *wa:r- "kid"	Som. waḥar-	Cush: phonol (ḥ)	
ptSNil *sike "mud, cow dung"	Galla dike "dried cow dung"; Som. digo- "cow dung"	ECush: distrib; phonol (ECush change d > s)	s for ECush *d

SOUTHERN NILOTIC	EASTERN CUSHITIC ATTESTATION	SOURCE	COMMENTS
ptSNil *api:ye (preSNil *api:rie) "large carnivore"	Galla ārba "elephant"; Yaaku arape "large feline"	Cush: distrib	preSNil *r
Dadog gidgido:d "very small tick"	Som. kudkude-, Saho kudkud "tick"	ECush: distrib	
ptKal *inser "louse"	Galla injeran; Somali injir; Konso ikira; Geleba izire	Cush: distrib	
ptKal *mo:so:ŋ "sorghum"	Galla misinga; Sid. mešinga	Cush: distrib; phonol (ECush change g, k > j)	
ptKal *mᵿra:ta:n "to circumcise" ptKal *muren (EVicpreSNil *mura) "warrior" Pokot ce:mɨryɔ:n (< *-mur-) "circumcised girl" Nandi murunyo "razor" Nandi murmur "to cut up small"	Galla mur- "to cut, to circumcise," murmur- "to cut up small"; Sid. mur- "to circumcise"	Cush: distrib; deriv (< ECush "to cut")	
Dadog habe:o:d (preSNil *(y)abe:ri) "swearing of oath or curse"	Galla abār-; Som. habaar-; Saho abar "to curse"	Cush: distrib	preSNil *r
Dadog hæ:lad- (< *yɛ:l-) "a well"	Galla eila; Som. ʕeel-; Saho ʕela	Cush: distrib; phonol (ʕ)	
ptSNil *lo "six"	Galla jā; Som. liḥ-; Sid. leʔe; Saho leḥ	Cush: distrib (also in SCush); phonol (ḥ, ʔ)	
ptSNil *tɪsap "seven"	Galla torba; Som. toddoba	ECush: distrib; phonol (ECush change d > s)	SNil s for ECush *d

III

SOUTHERN NILOTIC	EASTERN CUSHITIC ATTESTATION	SOURCE	COMMENTS
ptSNil *sisi:t "eight"	Galla sadeit; Som. siddeed-; Sid. sette	ECush: distrib; phonol (ECush change d > s); deriv (< ECush "three")	SNil s for ECush *d
ptSNil *sɔkɔ:l "nine"	Galla sagal; Som. sagaal-; Saho sagal	Cush: distrib	
ptSNil *taman "ten"	Som. toban-; Sid. tonne; Saho tamman	Cush: distrib (common Cush)	
ptSNil *tiktem "twenty"	Galla digdama	Cush: deriv (final element < Cush *tomon "ten")	
ptKal *sosom "thirty"	Galla sodoma; Som. soddon; Saho soddom	ECush: distrib; phonol (ECush change d > s); deriv (as for "twenty")	SNil s for ECush *d
ptSNil *artam "forty"	Galla afurtama; Som. afartan	Cush: distrib; deriv (as for "twenty")	
ptKal *kɔnɔm "fifty"	Galla šantama; Som. konton; Saho kontom	Cush: distrib; deriv (as for "twenty")	
Dadog la:dam "sixty"	Galla jātama; Som. lihdan; Saho lehatom	Cush: distrib; deriv (as for "twenty")	
Dadog se:dam "eighty"	Galla sadeitama; Som. siddeetan	Cush: distrib; deriv (as for 'twenty"),	
ptSNil *po:qol "hundred"	Som. boqol; Saho bol	Cush: distrib	

ORIGIN: Undetermined ancient Eastern Cushitic language; not Galla, Somali, or Saho, or direct ancestor language of any of these. Reason: ptECush *d >s (see numbers), a sound change which has not occurred in any of the three languages. The change of *d > z or s has occurred, though, in several Eastern Cushitic languages, for example, Sidamo and Konso. Time of borrowing: see Chapter 4.

VOCABULARY SOURCES:

(1) Proto–Southern Nilotic vocabulary items were reconstructed on the basis of vocabulary collected for several Southern Nilotic dialects by the writer or drawn from published sources. The following are the dialects utilized and the sources for each:

Barabaig (Dadog): Matayo Gidageney, about 25 years of age, and Gidornyesh, an old man of perhaps 70 years, both of the immediate neighborhood of Balangida Lelu, Tanzania.

Pokot (Kalenjin): Samwel, about 30 or 35 years of age, of Amudat, Uganda.

Kony (Kalenjin, Elgon): Reuben Masibai, about 25 years of age, and Mary, his wife, about 20 years of age, of Kimilili, Kenya.

Akie (Kalenjin, South): Petro Muhina, about 20 to 25 years of age, who grew up in Kijungu (Masai), Tanzania, but had been away from home for some years.

Tuken (Kalenjin, Nandian): Mathew arap Chebii, about 20 years of age, a student at University College, Nairobi, of Saimo (North Tuken dialect area), Baringo, Kenya.

Keyo (Kalenjin, Nandian): Francis arap Kigen, age in early 20's, a student at University College, Nairobi.

Nandi (Kalenjin, Nandian): A. C. Hollis, *The Nandi* (Oxford: Clarendon Press, 1909), and A. N. Tucker and M. A. Bryan, "Noun Classification in Kalenjin: Nandi and Kipsigis," *African Language Studies*, V (1964), VI (1965).

Kamelilo (Kalenjin, East): G. W. B. Huntingford, "Modern Hunters: Some Account of the Kamelilo-Kapchepkendi Dorobo (Okiek) of Kenya Colony," *Journal of the Royal Anthropological Institute*, LIX (1929).

(2) Eastern Cushitic vocabulary was drawn from the following sources:

Galla: Arnold W. Hodson and Craven H. Walker, *Elementary and Practical Grammar of the Galla or Oromo Language* (London: Society for Promoting Christian Knowledge, 1922).

Somali: Christopher R. V. Bell, *The Somali Language* (London: Longmans, 1953).

Sidamo: Martino M. Moreno, *Manuale di Sidamo* (Milan: A. Mondadori, 1940).

Saho: Leo Reinisch, *Die Saho-Sprache*, Vol. II (*Wörterbuch*) (Vienna: A. Holder 1889, 1890).

Yaaku: See Appendix H.2.

Southern Cushitic Loanwords in Proto–Southern Nilotic

SOUTHERN NILOTIC	SOUTHERN CUSHITIC ATTESTATION	SOURCE	COMMENTS
ptSNil *asi(:s) "sun"	ptSCush *aze-	SCush: distrib; phonol (z)	
ptKal *sɔ:i- (preSNil *sɔ:ri) "buffalo"	ptRift *sɔreʔ-; Ir. sareeʔa	SCush: distrib; phonol (ʔ)	SNil ɔ for WRift a
ptSNil *sapɪt- "porcupine"	ptWRift *sapat-	?	
ptSNil *lʸɔkɔ:t "to hunt"	ptWRift *hlakat	SCush: phonol (hl); deriv (< SCush "to shoot, pierce")	SNil ɔ for WRift a
ptSNil *qa:rʌ:man- "young man"	Bur. qaraymo; ptSCush *qar- "circumcised young person"	SCush: distrib; morphol (SCush n. suff. in -m-)	
ptSNil *panan "pauper"	ptIr *pan-	?	
ptSNil *sala:i- "twin"	ptWRift *tsar- "two"	SCush: phonol (ts)	
ptSNil *sorem-/*sɔrem- "scarification"	Bur. saar- "to scarify"	SCush: morphol (SCush n. suff. -em-)	SNil o or ɔ for WRift a

Possible Members of the Loanword Set

Dadog dæ:re:m- "magician"	ptRift daˤar- "to work magic"	SCush: phonol (ˤ); morphol (SCush n. suff. -em-). Not WRift: specif. form, meaning not attested	
Dadog še:d "moon"	ptSCush *hleh-; ptWRift *hleheŋ	SCush: distrib; phonol (hl) (h). Not WRift: specif. shape	SNil *lʸ for SCush hl, as in "to hunt"

ORIGIN: Southern Cushitic language belonging to the Rift branch; not West Rift language. Reasons: (1) most of attestations are from Rift languages only; (2) not West Rift because language still maintained *ɔ, which had already fallen together with *a in proto–West Rift. Time of borrowing: at least proto–Southern Nilotic period, but began in at least late pre–Southern Nilotic times because word "buffalo" lacks the r lost at the end of that period.

COMPARISON: Source language probably ancestor of or very closely related to sources of loanwords of Appendixes B.3–B.5. Reason: similar phonetic feature, ɔ for some West Rift a.

SPECIAL POINTS: Dadog words added at end of appendix suggested as words that possibly belonged to set but now are found only in Dadog, because they are of Southern Cushitic origin but not of West Rift origin, as are all the rest of the Southern Cushitic loanwords in Dadog. They could indicate independent Dadog contacts, however.

VOCABULARY SOURCES:
(1) For Southern Nilotic vocabulary items see Appendix B.1.
(2) Proto–Southern Cushitic, proto-Rift, and proto–West Rift vocabulary items were reconstructed largely on the basis of vocabulary collected by the writer for four Southern Cushitic languages and published materials on the other three known Southern Cushitic languages. The four languages and the sources for each are the following:
Iraqw: Afraim Hayuma, about 20 years of age, a student at University College, Nairobi, in 1967; grew up at Mbulu, Tanzania.
Burungi: Damas Dinya, about 30 years of age, of Goima (Kondoa), Tanzania.
Mbugu: Aloisi Pius Kidara, about 20 years of age, and Benedikt Hwayi Munga, 25 or 30 years old, both of Magamba (Lushoto), Tanzania.
Dahalo: Hagalana Wajaru, a woman of about 70 years; was born and grew up near Witu, Kenya.
Material on an additional Southern Cushitic language, *Alagwa*, was drawn from W. H. Whiteley, *A Short Description of Item Categories in Iraqw* (Kampala: East African Institute of Social Research, 1958). For a sixth language, *Aramanik*, short vocabularies appear in R. A. Maguire, "Il-Torōbo," *Journal of the African Society*, XXVII (1928), and in M. Merker, *Die Masai* (Berlin: D. Reimer, 1904). Unpublished information on a seventh language, *Qwadza*, was supplied very kindly by Peter Rigby.

Southern Cushitic Loanwords in Proto-Kalenjin

Proto-Kalenjin	Southern Cushitic Attestation	Source	Comments
*ɔr- "ashes"	ptSCush *ʕor-	SCush: distrib: phonol (ʕ)	
*mak- "hippopotamus"	ptWRift *max-	SCush: phonol (x)	
*-makɛ:t "hyena"	ptRift *mak- "wild animal"; cf. also Ma'a maɣa "rhinoceros" and maɣelu "game animal"	SCush: distrib; deriv	Kal suff. -t
*a:ra- "goat, sheep"	ptWRift *aara "goat"	?	
*seti:m "castrated he-goat"	ptWRift *tsata "barren animal"	SCush: phonol (ts); morphol (SCush n. suff. in m)	e for WRift a
*tɔm(p)ɛs "camel"	ptWRift *tsamas- "giraffe"	SCush: phonol	Kal ɔ for WRift a; Kal ɛ for WRift a
*sekem "bee"	?	SCush: morphol (SCush n. suff. -em-)	
*saka:s "to hunt, to collect food"	?	SCush: morphol (SCush v. caus. suff. -VVs)	
*tɔ:i- "stranger"	ptWRift *dahay-	SCush: phonol (h) (d)	Kal ɔ for WRift a
*lɛkɛm "hill"	ptWRift *laq- "pointed object"	SCush: phonol (q); morphol (SCush n. suff. -em-)	Kal ɛ for WRift a
*lɛ:kɛ "white-and-dark-flecked	Ir. laqɛ "ash-flecked cow"	SCush: phonol (q)	Kal ɛ for WRift a

Proto-Kalenjin	Southern Cushitic Attestation	Source	Comments
*ta:e: "copper wire"	Ir. ta^ʕi "copper neck ring"	SCush: phonol (ʕ)	
*tui "to pound grain"	ptSCush *tuʔ-	SCush: distrib	
*porok "palm wine"	ptWRift *buura "beer"	SCush: phonol (b)	Kal suff. -k
*te:rɪ:t "dust"	ptSCush *teeri	SCush: distrib	Kal suff. -t
*su:pet "wooden arrow" / *su:pen "log"	Bur. supay "wooden arrow"	?	Kal suff. -t, -n
*co:k- "sword and sheath"	Bur. coqiya, pl. coqay "iron spike"	? SCush: phonol (q)	
*kɛ:n "mortar"	ptWRift *kun-	SCush: deriv (< stem of other words dealing with grain)	*ɛ for WRift *u
*kɛnɛ:r "hyrax"	ptWRift *kuun-	SCush: morphol (SCush n. suff. in r)	*ɛ for WRift *u

ORIGIN: Rift Southern Cushitic language not belonging to West Rift subgroup. Reasons: see Appendix B.2. Time of borrowing: between end of proto–Southern Nilotic and end of proto-Kalenjin periods.

COMPARISON: Source language probably especially closely related to sources of loanwords of Appendixes B.2, B.4, and B.5. Reason: similar phonetic features, ɔ and ɛ for some West Rift a.

SPECIAL POINTS: A few of the words may actually go back to the proto– and pre–Southern Nilotic borrowing period of the words of Appendix B.2, but are found now only in Kalenjin dialects.

VOCABULARY SOURCES:
(1)   Kalenjin: see Appendix B.1.
(2)   Southern Cushitic: see Appendix B.2.

Restricted Southern Cushitic Loanwords in Kalenjin

KALENJIN	SOUTHERN CUSHITIC ATTESTATION	SOURCE	COMMENTS
Nandi *tukatuk* "doorpost"	Iraqw *duuxutamo,* pl. *duuxutee*	SCush: phonol (*x*) (*d*)	
Nandi *inkor* "leather clothing"	Iraqw *inqwar* "leather cape"	SCush: phonol (*q*)	Kal *o* for WRift *a* ?
Nandi *solkoi* "kudu"	Cf. Iraqw *sargi* "gazelle"	?	If valid, Kal *o* for WRift *a*
ptNandian **su:mei* "men's hairdo"	ptRift **seʔem-* "hair of head, men's hairdo"	SCush: distrib; phonol (?); morphol (SCush n. suff. in *-m-*)	Kal *u* for Rift *eʔe*
Nandi *sepet,* Keyo *sapta* "half gourd"	Iraqw *seepay* "small calabash"	?	Kal suff. *-t*
Kony *ya:mɛ* "floor"	ptWRift **yaam-* "floor, yard"	SCush: distrib	
Nandi-Kony **saram-* "twin"	ptWRift **tsar-* "two"	SCush: morphol (SCush pl. n. suff. *-am-*)	

ORIGIN: See Appendix B.3. Time of borrowing: uncertain; Nandi has a few more Southern Cushitic loanwords unique to itself than other Kalenjin dialect groups have but not enough to determine that these represent a post–proto-Kalenjin borrowing period.

COMPARISON: Source language probably especially closely related to source of loanwords of Appendixes B.2, B.3, and B.5. Reason: similar phonetic feature, ɔ for some West Rift *a*.

VOCABULARY SOURCES:
  (1) *Nandi, Keyo, Kony:* see Appendix B.1.
  (2) *Iraqw* and proto–West Rift: see Appendix B.2.

B.5

Southern Cushitic Loanwords in Gusii

GUSII	SOUTHERN CUSHITIC ATTESTATION	SOURCE	COMMENTS
ricɔɛ, pl. *ama-* "beeswax"	Bur. *caˤiya*, pl. *caˤo* "honeycomb"	SCush: phonol (ˤ); morphol (lack B pref.)	Gusii ɔ for WRift *a*
ekunu, pl. *ci-* "mortar"	ptWRift **kun-*	SCush: distrib; morphol (lack B pref.)	
nyasanako "black-and-white-splotched cow"	Ir. *sanakʷ* "black-and-white or black-and-red-splotched cow"	SCush: phonol (*kʷ*); morphol (lack B pref.)	
-sɛrɛɛt- "to thatch"	Ir. *tsarami*, pl. *tsarai* "thatch"	SCush: phonol (*ts*); morphol (SCush v. ext. *-VVt-*)	Gusii ɛ for WRift *a*
-saat- "to scarify"	prWRift **tsaat-* "to cut"	SCush: distrib; phonol (*ts*)	
ɛkɛnɛɛra "small tick"	Ir. *ineeramo*, pl. *ineera*	?	

ORIGIN: See Appendix B.3.

COMPARISON: Source language not same language as for Appendix B.3 but probably closely related. Reason: has some similar phonetic features, namely ɔ and ɛ for some West Rift *a*, but also one difference, *u* for West Rift *u* in "mortar," where "mortar" in B.3 had ɛ.

VOCABULARY SOURCES:
(1) *Gusii:* Henry Bikeri, age in early 20's, a student at University College, Nairobi; of Nyaguta (Kisii), Kenya.
(2) Southern Cushitic: see Appendix B.2.

West Rift Cushitic Loanwords in Dadog

DADOG	WEST RIFT ATTESTATION	SOURCE	COMMENTS
saqwæ:la:d "snare trap"	Ir. *tsaxweeli*	Ir: phonol (*ts*)	
næ:mo:d "wildcat"	Gor. *naˀamo*	Ir: phonol (?)	
li:ndamo:d "bushbuck"	Gor. *ilintimo*	Ir: morphol (SCush n. suff. in -*m*-)	
uma:li:d "hedgehog"	ptWRift **umaali*	WRift: distrib	
gu:di:d "mole"	ptWRift **kut-*; ptIr **kuti*	WRift: distrib. Ir: specif. shape (Bur. has *kutia*, Alagwa *kutumo*)	
diæ:mæ:nd, pl. *diæ:maig* "cattle egret"	Ir. *deˀeemi*	Ir: morphol (SCush v. ext. -VV*m*-); deriv (SCush "to herd")	
do:do:d "calf pen"	Ir. *ditoˀo*	Ir: phonol (?)	*o* for Ir. *i* by assimil. to following *o:*
sime:d "watering trough dug in ground"	ptWRift **simet-* "puddle"; Ir. *simet* "wooden watering trough"	WRift: distrib. Ir: specif. meaning	
kunio:d "mortar"	ptWRift **kun-*; ptIr **kune*	WRift: distrib. Ir: specif. shape	
muse:d "pestle"	ptWRift **mays-*; ptIr **mus-*	WRift: distrib. Ir: specif. shape	
gagan- "to weed"	Ir. *kakaanuus-*	?	
mæ:ngure: "red sorghum"	Ir. *mangwaree* (ptSCush **magale* "sorghum")	SCush: distrib	
lo:si "beans"	ptWRift **lo(n)si*; Ir. *losi*	WRift: distrib. Ir: specif. shape	

DADOG	WEST RIFT ATTESTATION	SOURCE	COMMENTS
gasi:s "potato, yam"	Ir. *kasiis* "sweet potato"	Ir: pattern (other Dadog n. without sec. suff. also recent loans)	
fayu:d "arrow shaft"	ptWRift **fayu* "arrow"	WRift: distrib	Only in Bur., Alagwa; but diff. meaning in Dadog
so:li:d "blunt wooden arrow"	Bur. *ʕensolay*	WRift: phonol (ʕ)	
sirbi:d "waterpot"	ptWRift **sirib-*; Bur. *sibida*; ptIr **sirwi*	WRift: distrib. Ir: specif. shape	Borrowed from preIr before ptWRift **b > w*
o:gu:gu:d "calabash pulp and seeds"	Bur. *okuku* "heap of weeds, rubbish"	?	Diff. meaning in Dadog
dæ:re:d "ashes"	Ir. *daʕara*	Ir: phonol (ʕ); deriv (< Ir. *daʕ-* "to burn")	
ag- "to eat"	ptWRift **ag-/*ʕag-*; ptIr **ʕay-*; ptSCush **ag-/*ʕag-*	SCush: distrib; phonol (ʕ). Not late ptIr: specif. shape (**g > y*)	

ORIGIN: An Iraqwan dialect. Reason: words generally are either attested only in Iraqwan, or are closest in shape to Iraqwan forms, or are different in meaning or shape from the words in the non-Iraqwan West Rift languages, Burungi and Alagwa.

VOCABULARY SOURCES:
    (1) *Dadog:* see Appendix B.1.
    (2) West Rift: see Appendix B.2.

Southern Cushitic Loanwords in Akie

AKIE	SOUTHERN CUSHITIC ATTESTATION	SOURCE	COMMENTS
panko:ku: "cave"	?	ERiftSCush; morphol (ERift n. suff. *-ku, -ko*)	Ultim < B (EastnB **pango*)
cayko: "lesser kudu"	?	ERift: morphol (ERift n. suff. *-ku, -ko*)	
kilitue:, pl. *kilito:* "digging stick"	?	ERift: morphol (ERift n. suff. *-tu, -to*)	
pipiyɛ:tu, pl. *pipiyɛ:ra* "heel"	?	ERift: morphol (ERift n. suff. *-tu, -to*) (ERift n. pl. suff. *-era*)	
kantatu: "anklebone"	?	ERift: morphol (ERift n. suff. *-tu, -to*)	
sɛkɛtɛtia:ntɛ:, pl. *sɛkɛtɛtik* "charcoal"	Dah. *nsikitsa*	ERift: morphol (2nd *t* = ERift n. suff. *-tu, -to* ?)	

ORIGIN: An East Rift Southern Cushitic language. Reason: morphological fossils in loan-words in Akie. Time of borrowing: since the end of the proto-Kalenjin period.

VOCABULARY SOURCES:

(1) *Akie*: see Appendix B.1.
(2) Southern Cushitic: see Appendix B.2.

Appendixes C.1–C.3

Southern Nilotic Loanword Sets
in Southern Cushitic

C.1

Dadog Loanwords in Aramanik

ARAMANIK	DADOG ATTESTATION	SOURCE	COMMENTS
sāmag, sāma "three"	*samag-* (ptSNil *somok)	SNil: distrib. Dadog: specif. shape (*a*)	
mūt "five"	*mu:d* (ptSNil **mu:t*)	SNil: distrib. Dadog: pattern ("three," "six," "seven" < Dadog)	Dadog *mu:d* realized as *mu:t*
la "six"	*la* (ptSNil *lo)	SNil: distrib. Dadog.: specif. shape (*a*)	
isuba "seven"	*isba* (ptSNil *tɪsap)	SNil: distrib. Dadog: specif. shape (loss of initial *t*)	
giāiesuk "giraffe"	Cf. *qæid* ?	? SNil: morphol (SNil n. suff. in *s*)	

VOCABULARY SOURCES:
(1) *Aramanik:* see Appendix B.2.
(2) *Dadog:* see Appendix B.1.

C.2

Dadog Loanwords in Iraqwan

IRAQW, GOROWA	DADOG ATTESTATION	SOURCE	COMMENTS
Ir. *gamboot*, pl. *gambu* "shield"	*igæ:mbo:d*	Dadog: morphol (SNil sec. suff. in *t*)	
Ir. *mayšot*, pl. *mayšu* "sack"	*mišo:d* (ptSNil **mɪlʸo(:t)*)	SNil: distrib; morphol (SNil sec. suff. in *t*). Dadog: specif. shape (*š* for ptSNil **lʸ*)	
Ir. *soono* "barren cow"	ptSNil **so:no-* (preSNil)	SNil: distrib	
Ir. *daamo* "beard"	*da:mo:g* (ptSNil **ta:mo-*)	SNil: distrib. Dadog: specif. shape (*d* for SNil **t*)	
Ir. *duaqedamo*, pl. *duaqee* (< **dawaqed-*) "Masai"	*dæbæ:qjæ:nd*, pl. *dæbæ:qe:g*	Dadog: morphol (SNil n. pl. suff. in *t*)	Borrowed before preIr **b* > ptIr **w*
Ir. *hagitee* "Hatsa people"	*ha:ge:di:g* (ptSNil **(y)a:k-* "hunting people")	SNil: distrib; morphol (SNil n. pl. suff. in *t*). Dadog: specif. shape (*h* < ptSNil **y*)	
Gor. *dešgudi* a kind of antelope	*ude:šqu:d* "roan antelope"	Dadog: deriv (< Dadog "white mouth")	
Gor. *sasodi* "gazelle"	*šæ:šo:d* "Thomson's gazelle"	Dadog: phonol (*š*); morphol (SNil sec. suff. in *t*)	
Gor. *udanjijiri* "pangolin"	+*udanjir-*	Dadog: deriv (Dadog deriv pref. *ud(a)-*)	

VOCABULARY SOURCES:

(1) *Iraqw:* see Appendix B.1; *Gorowa:* G. H. Swynnerton, "Vernacular Names of Some of the Better-known Mammals in the Central Province, Tanganyika," *Tanganyika Notes and Records*, No. 21 (1946).

(2) *Dadog:* see Appendix B.1. The word preceded by a plus (+) is drawn from Swynnerton, *op. cit.*

Kalenjin Loanwords in Aramanik

ARAMANIK	KALENJIN ATTESTATION	SOURCE	COMMENTS
kirigit "bull"	ptSNil **kiru:k*, ptKal **kiru:k*, ptKal with sec. suff. **kirkit*	SNil: distrib; morphol (SNil sec. suff. in *t*). Kal: specif. shape	
kitokog "wooden bowl"	ptKal **tɔ:kei*, Pokot meaning = "wooden barrel," Tuken = "tightly woven cup"	Kal: distrib; morphol (Nil pref. *ki-*)	
magadeg, pl. *magadaig* "leather clothing"	ptKal **makata*	Kal: distrib; morphol (lack Aram. suff.)	
tamašiet, pl. *tamagig* "woman's brass earring"	Nandi *tamokyo*, pl. *tamok* "finger ring"	Kal: morphol (lack Aram. suff.)	*a* for Nandi *o* = Kal **ɔ*?
kiruakidet "governing elder"	ptKal **ki:ruɔ:ki:n*; Akie *ki:rua:ke:*	Kal: morphol (SNil sec. suff. in *t* = *d* of Aram. form); deriv (< Kal "to advise"). SKal: specif. shape (*a* for Kal *ɔ*, lack Kal final *n* of stem)	*a* for Kal **ɔ*; lacks stem-final *n* of ptKal
ebindadet "age set"	ptKal **ɪpɪn*	Kal: distrib; morphol (SNil sec. suff. in *t* = -(*da*)*d*- of Aram. form)	
kisirijo "leader of age-set band"	Nandi *sirit* "age-set band"	Kal: morphol (SNil n. suff. *-io* = *-jo* < **-tio*)	*-io* for Kal **iɔ(:n)*
olgoiatiki "medicine man"	ptKal **ɔ:rkɔ:yɔ(:n)*	Kal: distrib; morphol (SNil sec. suff. in *t*) (lack Aram. suff.)	*o* for Kal **ɔ*; *-ia* for Kal **-iɔ(:n)*; *l* for **r* is probably error

ARAMANIK	KALENJIN ATTESTATION	SOURCE	COMMENTS
šogoto "witch"	ptKal *sa:kut "to bewitch"	Kal: distrib; deriv (see B.7)	š for Kal *s
sanyeg "lover (male)" sanyet "lover (female)"	ptKal *sa:nia "lover" (preSNil *sa:n- "friend")	SNil: distrib; morphol (SNil n. suff. -ia). Kal: specif. meaning	

ORIGIN: Undetermined Kalenjin dialect or dialects. Reason: some features of some words (a for ɔ in "woman's earring," "governing elder") suggest South Kalenjin provenance; other features (o for Kal ɔ in "medicine man," "leader of age-set band") suggest non–South Kalenjin origin for the words. Time of borrowing: since the end of the proto-Kalenjin period and before the rise of Masai influence in Tanzania Masailand.

SPECIAL POINTS: Evidence on Aramanik is so inadequate and so inadequately recorded when it has been collected that the question of the origin of the above loanword set cannot yet be answered.

VOCABULARY SOURCES:
    (1) *Aramanik:* see Appendix B.2.
    (2) Kalenjin: see Appendix B.1.

Appendixes D.1–D.15

Southern Nilotic Loanword Sets in Bantu

D.1

Southern Nilotic Loanwords in East Victoria Bantu

Proto-EVicB	Southern Nilotic Attestation	Source	Comments
*-sɛkɛ "beer straw"	ptKal *sek-	SNil: morphol (lack B pref.)	k for SNil k or q
*-suuji "wild dog"	ptSNil *su:i-	SNil: morphol (lack B pref.)	
*-subeeni "young ewe"	ptKal *supe:n (preSNil *supe:n)	SNil: distrib; morphol (lack B pref.)	
*-saasaba (var. Kuria -sansaba) "six"	ptSNil *tɪsap "seven" (< preSNil)	SNil: distrib; morphol (lack B pref.)	EVicB s for SNil t; EVicB a for SNil i; Kuria prenasalized consonant after sV-
*-eeri (var. Gusii -ɛɛri) "male bovine"	ptSNil *(y)e:i-; preSNil *e:ri	SNil: distrib; morphol (lack B pref.)	preSNil r
*-suunu "barren cow"	ptSNil *so:no	SNil: morphol (lack B pref.)	
*-sɛɛrɔ "hide"	Pokot sara "sheepskin"	SNil: morphol (lack B pref.)	
*-sikiri "donkey"	Dadog dige:d (preSNil *tike:ri)	SNil: pattern (s for *t)	s for SNil *t; k for SNil *k; preSNil *r retained

ORIGIN: Pre–Southern Nilotic language. Reason: retains r lost in proto–Southern Nilotic.

COMPARISON: Source language closely related to source languages of loanwords of Appendixes D.2–D.4. Reasons: (1) location of borrowing languages all in same general region today; (2) interlocking set of common phonetic features—preSNil r retained (D.1, D.3, D.4); s for some Southern Nilotic t (D.1, D.3, D.4); prenasalized stop after sV- (D.1–D.4); a for Southern Nilotic ɔ (D.2, D.4); a for some Southern Nilotic i (D.1–D.3).

Vocabulary sources:

    (1)   Proto–East Victoria Bantu words were reconstructed on the basis of their occurrence in Bantu dialects located on the east of Lake Victoria both north and south of the Kavirondo Gulf. The dialects chiefly studied and their sources are the following:

    Gusii: see Appendix B.5.

    Jita: Faustine Luzangi, age in early 20's, a student at University College, Nairobi; of mainland portion Ukerewe Area, Tanzania.

    Idakho: James Lugonzo, about 40 years old, of Kakamega, Kenya.

    Bukusu: Henry Mwambu, age about 30 years, and David Tyetye, similar age, of Kimilili, Kenya. Supplementary evidence from Kwaya, Kuria, and Shashi was also utilized; sources of this material were as follows:

    Shashi: Harry H. Johnston, "The Ki-Shashi Language (S.E. Victoria Nyanza)," *Journal of the African Society*, XIX (1920).

    Kwaya: Anthony Minangi, age in early 20's, a student at University College, Dar es Salaam.

    Kuria: Otto Dempwolff, "Beiträge zur Kenntnis der Sprachen in Deutsch-Ostafrika: 4. Kulia," *Zeitschrift für Kolonialsprachen*, V (1914–15).

    (2)   Southern Nilotic: see Appendix B.1.

Special points: Proto–East Victoria Bantu probably consisted of a cluster of dialects, variously ancestral to the different East Victoria Bantu languages, rather than a single ancient Bantu dialect. Peoples speaking some of the dialects early moved northward and became the ancestors of the Bantu of the North and Central Nyanza and Mount Elgon regions; others remained south of the Kavirondo Gulf and became the ancestors of the Gusii, Kwaya, Zanaki, *et al.*

Southern Nilotic Loanwords in Southeast Victoria Bantu

Proto-SEVicB	Southern Nilotic Attestation	Source	Comments
*-ka "home"	ptSNil *qɔ "house"	SNil: phonol (q); morphol (lack B pref.)	SEVicB a for SNil ɔ; k for SNil q. But cf. EastnB *-ka "wife" ?
*-saani "friend"	ptKal *sa:n- "lover"	SNil: morphol (lack B pref.)	
*-mura "young man, boy"	ptKal *muren "warrior"	SNil: morphol (lack B pref.)	See B.1
*-subaati "young woman"	Dadog sube:d "most recent wife"	SNil: morphol (SNil sec. suff. in t) (lack B pref.)	
*-muuma "oath"	ptKal *mu:m-	SNil: morphol (lack B pref.)	
*-saariiru "hawk"	ptKal *si:rere	SNil: morphol (lack B pref.)	EVicB a for SNil i
*-gɔrɔɛ (var. Gusii -gɔrɛ'ɛ, Jita -koroohe) "he-goat"	Dadog qwarai:d	SNil: phonol (q); morphol (lack B pref.)	Dadog a often < *o; SEVicB g for SNil q, except Jita k for q
*-saakua (var. Gusii -sankua) "sheepskin"	?	SNil: morphol (SNil suff. -ua)	Gusii pre-nasalized consonant after sV-; k for presumed SNil k or q
*-maanua "kid, lamb"	?	SNil: morphol (SNil suff. -ua)	
Age-set names:			
*-nyangi	ptKal *nyɔ:nki	SNil: morphol (lack B pref.)	SEVicB a for SNil ɔ

Proto-SEVicB	Southern Nilotic Attestation	Source	Comments
*-maina	ptKal *maina		
*-cuuma	ptKal *cu:ma		
*-saai	ptKal *sɔ:we		SEVicB a for SNil ɔ
*-gorongoro	ptKal *koronkoro		SEVicB g for SNil k

ORIGIN: See Appendix D.1.

COMPARISON: See Appendix D.1.

VOCABULARY SOURCES:

    (1) Proto–Southeast Victoria Bantu words are reconstructed on the basis of vocabulary items collected for *Gusii*, *Jita*, *Kwaya*, *Kuria*, and *Shashi*. For sources of these see Appendix D.1.

    (2) Southern Nilotic: see Appendix B.1.

Southern Nilotic Loanwords in Gusii

GUSII	SOUTHERN NILOTIC ATTESTATION	SOURCE	COMMENTS
esindakɛ, pl. *ci-* "needle"	ptSNil *sʌtek*	SNil: distrib; morphol (lack B pref.)	Gusii prenasalized consonant after *s*V-; *k* for SNil *k*
risosa, pl. *ama-* "calabash plant"	ptKal *sot* "calabash"	SNil: morphol (lack B pref.)	EVicB *s* for SNil *t*
-bariri "red"	ptKal *piri:r*	SNil: distrib	EVicB *a* for SNil *i*; EVicB *b* for SNil *p*
ɛnkɔrɔmba, pl. *ci-* "mosquito"	Pokot *rimpə* (< *rumpo*)	SNil: morphol (SNil pref. *kɔ-*) (lack B pref.)	*k* for presumed SNil *k*
-abuus- "to sweep"	ptKal *pu:c*	SNil: morphol (initial *a-* = SNil v. pref. *i-* ?)	EVicB *a* for SNil *i* ?
ebaarate, pl. *ci-* "large knife"	Dadog *ba:rd*	SNil: morphol (SNil sec. suff. in *t*) (lack B pref.)	
omoreete, pl. *eme-* "side bedslat"	Dadog *mari:d* "bank, edge"	SNil: morphol (SNil sec. suff. in *t*)	Dadog *a* often from *o*
esaiga, pl. *ci-* "young men's house"	Dadog *sa:igi:d* "age set"	SNil: phonol (unusual for B); morphol (lack B pref.)	*g* for SNil *k*
ekeobiiria, pl. *ebi-* "rhinoceros"	Dadog *ho:burje:d* < *yo:buria*	SNil: morphol (SNil n. suff. *-ia*) (lack B pref.)	
ebaacua, pl. *ci-* "thigh"	?ptSNil *kupe:s-*	SNil: morphol (SNil n. suff. *-ua*)	
ebaasweti "python"	?	SNil: morphol (SNil n. suff. *-ua*) (SNil sec. suff. in *t*)	

Gusii	Southern Nilotic Attestation	Source	Comments
ekemiinca, pl. ebi- "tail"	?	SNil: morphol (ca = form of SNil n. suff. -ia)	
etuukia "hair of head"	?	SNil: morphol (SNil n. suff. -ia)	k for presumed *k or *q
egetunua, pl. ebi- "mountain"	? ptSNil *tulua "hill"	SNil: morphol (SNil n. suff. -ua)	
eritigere, pl. ama- "donkey"	Dadog dige:d (preSNil *tike:ri)	SNil: distrib; morphol (lack B pref.)	Retains preSNil *r; g for SNil *k
esike, pl. ci- "mud, including cow dung"	ptSNil *sike "mud, including cow dung"; ptKal *sik- "cow dung"	SNil: distrib; morphol (lack B pref.). Not Kal: specif. meaning	k for SNil *k

ORIGIN: See Appendix D.1.

COMPARISON: See Appendix D.1.

SPECIAL POINTS: The variance in stem shape of the entry *eritigere*, "donkey," from the common East Victoria Bantu *-sikiri* requires that a second pre–Southern Nilotic people (pre–Southern Nilotic *r* is retained in both forms), in addition to the Victoria pre–Southern Nilotes, have influenced at least the linguistic ancestors of the Gusii. Note also that *-tigere* has *g* where other words in the appendix have *k* for Southern Nilotic *k*. Might inconsistencies in Bantu rendering of Southern Nilotic *k* or *q* in Appendix D.2 be explained, too, by postulation of two pre–Southern Nilotic loanword sources rather than by assumption of sound changes in Victoria pre–Southern Nilotic dialects? The co-occurrence of the *-tigere* root in Sonjo and the lack of a *t > s* change in the more easterly pre–Southern Nilotic languages (e.g., Appendix D.8) would suggest a possible locus for this second pre–Southern Nilotic people to the east of the Victoria pre–Southern Nilotes.

VOCABULARY SOURCES:
(1) *Gusii:* see Appendix B.5.
(2) Southern Nilotic: see Appendix B.1.

Southern Nilotic Loanwords in Jita

Jita	Southern Nilotic Attestation	Source	Comments
intyaanyi, pl. *jin-* "animal"	ptSNil *tiɔ:ny*	SNil: distrib; morphol (lack B pref.) (SNil n. suff. in *-ny*, now unprodc)	SEVicB *a* for SNil ɔ
risisinyo, pl. *ama-* "heel"	ptSNil *titiny*	SNil: distrib; morphol (lack B pref.) (SNil n. suff. in *-ny*, now unprodc)	
ecikuiria, pl. *ebi-* "sandal"	ptSNil *kue:yɔ* (preSNil *kue:riɔ*)	SNil: distrib; morphol (SNil n. suff. *-ia*) (lack B pref.)	*k* for SNil *k*
ecisusi, pl. *ebi-* "calabash"	ptKal *sot*	SNil: morphol (lack B pref.)	
ecitukuru, pl. *ebi-* "a kind of basket"	ptSNil *toqol-* "honey container (sack)"	SNil: distrib; phonol (*q*); morphol (lack B pref.)	*k* for SNil *q*
omukaruka, pl. *aba-* "elder"	ptSNil *kɔ:rk-* "married adult"	SNil: distrib; morphol (lack B pref.)	SEVicB *a* for SNil ɔ
inyarusi, pl. *jiny-* a cow of a particular coloration (undetermined)	ptKal *ɔ:ru:s-/ *a:ru:s*	SNil: morphol (lack B pref.)	*a* for SNil ɔ
risekeanda, pl. *ama-* "bamboo"	ptSNil *te:q(ia:n)*	SNil: distrib; phonol (*q*); morphol (SNil n. suff. *-an*) (*da* = SNil sec. suff. in *t*) (lack B pref.)	EVicB *s* for SNil *t*; Jita *k* for SNil *q*
orusongoorua "hedge euphorbia"	?	SNil: morphol (SNil n. suff. *-ua*) (lack B pref.)	
oruyabia "milk storage pot"	?	SNil: morphol (SNil n. suff. *-ia*)	

Jita	Southern Nilotic Attestation	Source	Comments
riuusua "men's headdress worn at dances"	?	SNil: morphol (SNil n. suff. *-ua*)	
ecikootua, pl. *ebi-* "cow's 'heel'"	?	SNil: morphol (SNil n. suff. *-ua*)	*k* for presumed SNil *k or *q
Kwaya *ritoonyi*, pl. *amatoonyi* "vulture"	ptSNil **moto:ny* or **mɔtɔ:ny*	SNil: distrib; morphol (SNil n. suff. *-ny*, now unprodc)	SEVicB *a* for SNil *ɔ* (SNil *mɔ-* interprt. as B pref. **ma-*)
Kwaya *inguruki*, pl. *ginguruki* "ram"	ptSNil **kiru:k* "bull; male"	SNil: distrib; morphol (lack B pref.)	

ORIGIN: See Appendix D.1.

COMPARISON: See Appendix D.1.

VOCABULARY SOURCES:

(1) *Jita:* Faustine Luzangi, age in early 20's, a student at University College, Nairobi; of mainland Kerewe Area, Tanzania.

(2) Southern Nilotic: see Appendix B.1.

Southern Nilotic Loanwords in Chaga

CHAGA	SOUTHERN NILOTIC ATTESTATION	SOURCE	COMMENTS
isara "goat hide"	Pokot *sǝra* "goatskin" (< **sera*)	SNil: morphol (lack B pref.)	Chaga *a* for SNil *e*
suvana "young ewe"	ptKal **supe:n,* preSNil **supe:n-*	SNil: distrib	Chaga *a* for SNil *e*
msasarwe "individual banana"	ptKal **sɔ:sU:rUɔ* "ensete"	SNil: morphol (*-we* = form of SNil n. suff. *-ua*)	
sure "small milk calabash"	ptKal **sot* "calabash" (preSNil)	SNil: distrib	*r* for *t* is Chaga sound change
lela, pl. *milela* "white stone; ice, snow, on Kilimanjaro" *malela* "milk"	ptSNil **lʸe:lʸ-* "white"	SNil: distrib; phonol (*lʸ*)	

ORIGIN: Southern Nilotic language of uncertain affinities.

VOCABULARY SOURCES:

    (1) *Chaga*: Emil Müller, *Wörterbuch der Djaga-Sprache* (*Madjame-Mundart*) (Hamburg: Eckardt & Messtorff, 1947).

    (2) Southern Nilotic: see Appendix B.1.

D.6

Southern Nilotic Loanwords in Kikuyu

Kikuyu	Southern Nilotic Attestation	Source	Comments
ngaati "wildebeest"	ptSNil *ɪnqat	SNil: phonol (*q*)	Shared with Sonjo (see D.7)
huria "rhinoceros"	Dadog *ho:burje:d* (< *yo:buria*)	SNil: morphol (SNil n. suff. *-ia*)	Shared with Sonjo (see D.7)
ngɔŋɔkɔŋi "woodpecker"	ptSNil *kɔŋkɔŋ	SNil: distrib; phonol (Kik. epithetic ɔ to maintain CVCV pattern); morphol (lack B pref.)	
ndigiri "donkey"	Dadog *dige:d* (preSNil *tike:ri*)	SNil: distrib; morphol (lack B pref.)	Cf. "Donkey" in D.3 and D.7; retains preSNil *r*
ngeboto a drink made with cow's blood	ptSNil *ke:p(o:t) "vein, especially jugular vein of cow"	SNil: distrib; morphol (SNil sec. suff. in *t*) (lack B pref.)	
keoomo, pl. *ci-* a coloration of goats	ptKal *o:mo "dark brown"; ptSNil *o:m- "brown"	SNil: morphol (lack B pref.)	
motarakwa, pl. *me-* "juniper"	ptKal *tarakua	SNil: morphol (SNil n. suff. *-ua*) (lack B pref.)	
mothoothi, pl. *me-* "Phoenix reclinata"	ptKal *so:s-, sing. *so:siɔ(:n)	SNil: morphol (lack B pref.)	
motɔrɔthua, pl. *me-* a kind of tree	?	SNil: morphol (SNil n. suff. *-ua*)	
cuuma name of an early generation set	ptKal *cu:ma (preSNil)	SNil: distrib	

KIKUYU	SOUTHERN NILOTIC ATTESTATION	SOURCE	COMMENTS
mwangi one of the two alternate ruling sets	ptKal **nyɔ:nki* (preSNil)	SNil: distrib; morphol (Kik. can replace *ny* with *mw* by treating as if B pref.; but SNil can't change *mw* > *ny*)	*a* for SNil **ɔ*; Kik treated *ny* as pref., replaced it with *mo* = *mw*
maina one of the two alternate ruling sets	ptKal **maina* (preSNil)	SNil: distrib	
-tuum- "to dance certain dance connected with circumcision ceremonies"	ptSNil **tu:m* "dance; to dance"; ptKal **tu:m* "circumcision ceremony; to perform circumcision ceremonies"	SNil: distrib	Word also in Kamba
ngɔnyeeki "outward-turned eye"	ptSNil **kɔ:ŋ*, pl. **kɔ:ny-* "eye"	SNil: distrib; morphol (SNil pl. sec. suff. in *k*) (lack B pref.)	
ngɔŋɔɔrua "long column"	?	SNil: morphol (SNil n. suff. *-ua*)	

ORIGIN: Pre–Southern Nilotic language. Reasons: (1) pre–Southern Nilotic *r* lost in proto–Southern Nilotic retained in one word; (2) majority of words are of pre- or proto–Southern Nilotic origin, and the rest are not overwhelmingly found only in one of the two modern Southern Nilotic branches; (3) morphological difference in one word ("Phoenix reclinata").

VOCABULARY SOURCES:
    (1) *Kikuyu:* T. G. Benson, *Kikuyu-English Dictionary* (Oxford: Clarendon Press, 1964).
    (2) Southern Nilotic: see Appendix B.1

D.7

Southern Nilotic Loanwords in Sonjo

Sonjo	Southern Nilotic Attestation	Source	Comments
mburia "rhinoceros"	Dadog ho:burje:d (< *yo: buria)	SNil: morphol (SNil n. suff. -ia) (lack B pref.)	Shared with Kikuyu (see D.6)
ntyaany "animal"	ptSNil *tiɔ:ny	SNil: distrib; morphol (SNil n. suff. in ny, now unprodc)	a for SNil ɔ; shared with Jita, Kwaya, Shashi (see D.4)
nxaat "wildebeest"	ptSNil *ɪnqat	SNil: distrib; phonol (q)	Shared with Kikuyu (see D.6)
nseroot "eland"	Cf. ptKal *si:rua "of eland color"	? SNil: morphol (SNil sec. suff. in t ?)	
mayɛk "hartebeest"	Cf. Dadog mæ:yæ:nd "Grant's gazelle"	? SNil: morphol (SNil pl. sec. suff. in k ?)	
ndikel "donkey"	Dadog dige:d (preSNil *tike:ri)	SNil: morphol (lack B pref.)	Shared with Gusii (see D.3)
marɔny "vulture"	ptSNil *moto:ny	SNil: distrib	a for SNil *o; r for SNil *t
gisɛɛr "cowhide"	Pokot sɔra "skin" (< *ser-); Tuken kisɛ:r "hide as catch-cloth"	SNil: morphol (lack B pref.)	Shared with EVicB (see D.1)
ndaaxua "sheepskin"	?	SNil: morphol (SNil n. suff. -ua)	Shared with SEVicB (see D.2)
buxooman "honey; beer"	ptKal *ko:men, Dadog qamung "honey beer"; ptKal *ku:m- "honey"	SNil: distrib; morphol (SNil n. suff. -(a)n) (lack B pref.)	a for Kal *e

SONJO	SOUTHERN NILOTIC ATTESTATION	SOURCE	COMMENTS
lɔŋ "shield"	ptSNil *lɔːŋ*	SNil: distrib. Not Masai: lacks Mas pref.	
kiditiny "heel"	ptSNil *titiny*	SNil: distrib; morphol (lacks B pref.)	Shared with Jita (see D.4)
ŋeeŋ "salt lick"	ptKal *nyeːny/*ŋeːŋ*	SNil: distrib; phonol (usual for Kal but not B word to start in ŋ)	
esai, pl. *ma-* "tail"	Kony *saːntɛt*, pl. *saːik* "bushy end of cow's tail" (< *saːi-)	SNil: morphol (lack B pref.)	
muuma "oath"	ptKal *muːm-*	See "oath," D.2	Shared with SEVicB (see D.2)

ORIGIN: Undetermined pre–Southern Nilotic, possibly several sources; see Chapter 5: some items may be secondary borrowings from other Bantu languages; a few items may be recent loans from a Kalenjin dialect (cf. "salt lick" and "tail").

VOCABULARY SOURCES:

(1) *Sonjo:* Naiman, about 25 years of age, of Samonge village (Masai), Tanzania, and Mangarisha Kokia, same age, of Oldoinyo Sambu (Masai), Tanzania.
(2) Southern Nilotic: see Appendix B.1.

D.8

Southern Nilotic Loanwords in Bantu Languages of Central West Tanzania

BANTU	SOUTHERN NILOTIC ATTESTATION	SOURCE	COMMENTS
General W&SW Tanz. B *-lugu "war"	ptSNil *luk- "raid"	SNil: morphol (lack B pref.)	
General W&SW Tanz. B *-lugaluga "soldier"			
General W&WC Tanz. B *-laala "gazelle"	Dadog šæ:šo:d (< *lʸa:lʸ-)	SNil: phonol (lʸ)	
Nyamwezi, Irangi *-lili "cowhide"	Kal *irir- "skin"	SNil: morphol (lack B pref.)	
Sangu, some Nyamwezi *-kwauŋando "hare"		SNil: morphol (SNil n. suff. -an) (-do = SNil sec. suff. in t)	Ultim < WRift *kwaʕaŋw
Hehe sengere "zebra"	Dadog si:ngi:ye:d (preSNil *si:nki:ri)	?	Hehe retains r

ORIGIN: Pre–Southern Nilotic language. Reasons: (1) pre–Southern Nilotic r lost in proto–Southern Nilotic is retained in "zebra"; (2) borrowed forms are neither typically Kalenjin nor typically Dadog in shape, and include one word, at least, not found in either modern Southern Nilotic branch.

VOCABULARY SOURCES:
Southern Nilotic: see Appendix B.1.

D.9

Southern Nilotic Loanwords in Proto–Luhyia-Gishu

Proto–Luhyia-Gishu	Southern Nilotic Attestation	Source	Comments
*kibeu "rhinoceros"	ptKal *kɪpєʊ	SNil: phonol (non-B shape -eu); morphol (Nil n. pref. ki-)	
*-taiyua "rooster"	ptKal *ta:iyua "spur fowl"	SNil: morphol (SNil suff. -ua) (lack B pref.)	
*-bay- "to keep cattle"	ptKal *pai	SNil: morphol (lack B v. affixes)	
*-lat- "to castrate"	ptKal *la:t	SNil: morphol (lack B v. affixes)	
*-sac- "to churn"	ptSNil *sac-	SNil: distrib	
*-aiyua "ax"	ptKal *a:iyua	SNil: morphol (SNil n. suff. -ua) (lack B pref.)	
*-uuc- "to fan"	ptKal *u:s	SNil: morphol (lack B v. affixes)	c for Kal *s
*-nab- "to sew"	ptSNil *na:p	SNil: distrib	
*-muka "calabash"	Pokot mu:kə	SNil: morphol (lack B pref.)	
*-libua "homestead gate"	?ptKal *ri:p "to guard"	SNil: morphol (SNil n. suff. -ua)	
*(mu)ŋolî "diviner"	ptKal *ŋo:r "to divine"	SNil: phonol (l) (ŋ = typical SNil init. consonant)	
*-saay- "to pray"	ptKal *sa:i	SNil: distrib (common Nil root)	
*-sooleeli "youth not yet of marriageable age"	Dadog so:ræ:ld "barren cow"	SNil: morphol (lack B pref.)	

ORIGIN: It is useful to consider the loanword sets of Appendixes D.9, D.10, and D.11 together. For both Appendixes D.9 and D.11 the source language of the loanwords was obviously very closely related to Kalenjin. In both shape and meaning similarities, the words of these sets attest this closeness. But there are also a number of significant differences between some words of the sets, especially the set in Appendix D.11, and their cognate forms in the Kalenjin dialects: (1) words with quite different meanings in the Bantu versions from those in the Kalenjin versions ("rooster," D.9, and "open forest," D.11); (2) words with different Southern Nilotic affixation in Bantu than in Kalenjin ("hawk," "hyrax," and "cow dung" in D.11); (3) *e* for *a* in certain of the Southern Nilotic *-ia, -ua* noun suffixes ("juniper," "cow dung" in D.11); (4) phonological differences in Bantu forms not explainable on rules of Bantu sound change ("to fan," D.9, and "partition," "open forest," D.11); (5) presence in sets of Appendixes D.9 and D.11 of Southern Nilotic loanwords not attested in any modern Southern Nilotic dialect ("homestead gate," D.9, and "bull," "capon," "leather sack," and "potsherd," D.11).

Thus the sources were dialects which were not clearly identifiable as Kalenjin; probably instead they should be seen as sister dialects of proto-Kalenjin spoken westward from proto-Kalenjin proper, and which followed their own evolution and development of dialects. From their location between Mount Elgon and the Kavirondo Gulf they may collectively be termed Kitoki Southern Nilotic. The source of the loanword set of Appendix D.11 may well have been a descendant dialect of the source of the set of Appendix D.9. That the differences from Kalenjin forms should be more pronounced in Appendix D.11 is to be expected, because the loanword set of Appendix D.11 is more recent than the set of Appendix D.9, and so more differences would have had time to develop between the period of the separation of the ancestors of the Kalenjin from those of the Kitoki Southern Nilotes and the period of loan activity.

Appendix D.10 appears to contain a mixed set of loanwords. Some words, such as "hoe," are clearly late borrowings from a Nandian dialect; but others, such as "knife," "savanna," and "juniper," were borrowed earlier. These three words must all have been borrowed before *r* became a phoneme in Bantu dialects because, in each, Southern Nilotic *r* has been replaced with *l*, or original *t* with *r* (*r* in these Bantu dialects developed out of *t*). The development of the *r* phoneme apparently began after dialects had already appeared in Luhyia and Gishu, but still very early because the sound change has spread to nearly all the dialects since that time. The word "savanna" in particular is probably from Kitoki Southern Nilotic because it has virtually the same meaning—different from the Kalenjin meaning for the word—as the related word (see under "open forest") in Appendix D.11.

VOCABULARY SOURCES:

(1) Bantu (Luhyia-Gishu): see under *Idakho* and *Bukusu* in Appendix D.1.
(2) Southern Nilotic: See Appendix B.1, as also for words in Appendixes D.10 and D.11.

D.10

Southern Nilotic Loanwords in Idakho

IDAKHO	SOUTHERN NILOTIC ATTESTATION	SOURCE	COMMENTS
ikilixi "bull"	ptSNil **kiru:k*	SNil: distrib; morphol (lack B pref.)	**g* for SNil **k*
liyoosi, pl. *ma-* "old cow"	ptKal **yo:s-*	SNil: distrib; morphol (lack B pref.)	
inkoote "camel"	Nandi *ingotio* "giraffe"	?	*t* maintained
mokombeeti "hoe"	ptNd **moko:mpe*	SNil: morphol (SNil sec. suff. in *t*)	*t* maintained
xitaabo "wooden bowl"	ptNd **ta:po*	SNil: morphol (lack B pref.)	*t* maintained
momanani "poor man"	ptSNil **panan*	SNil: distrib	SNil *p* assimil. to nasal, > *m*
ilotua "knife"	ptKal **ro:tua*	SNil: distrib; morphol (SNil n. suff. *-ua*)	Id. *l* for SNil *r*; but Wanga has apparently *r*
boriimo "savanna"	ptSNil **ti:m* "forest, bush"	SNil: distrib; morphol (lack B pref.)	*r* for SNil *t*
motalakua "juniper"	ptKal **tara:kua*	SNil: distrib; morphol (SNil n. suff. *-ua*)	*l* for SNil *r*
moluuminti, pl. *ba-* "enemy"	ptKal **ru:m* "to murder, to kill fellow tribesman of speaker"	SNil: distrib; morphol (SNil agent n. suff. *-in*) (SNil sec. suff. in *t*) (lack B pref.)	*l* for SNil *r*

D.11

Southern Nilotic Loanwords in Bukusu

BUKUSU	SOUTHERN NILOTIC ATTESTATION	SOURCE	COMMENTS
siciimi, pl. *bi-* "open forest"	ptSNil **ti:m* "forest, bush"	SNil: distrib; morphol (lack B pref.)	*c* for SNil *t* before front vowel
luteeka, pl. *n-* "bamboo"	ptSNil **te:q(ia:n)* (Nandi *te:ka*)	SNil: distrib; phonol: (*q*)	
kumutarakwe, pl. *kimi-* "juniper"	ptKal **tara:kua*	SNil: distrib; morphol (*-we* = form of SNil n. suff. *-ua*) (lack B pref.)	*r* for SNil **r*
kumutoboosua, pl. *kimi-* a kind of tree	Kony *tapɔswɛt*	SNil: morphol (SNil n. suff. *-ua*) (lack B pref.)	
simiyu "Sept.-Feb. dry season"	ptKal **kemeu*	SNil: deriv (< Kal "to eat"; basic sense = "hunger season")	*i* for Kal **e*; Buk. *si* < **ki-*
enkenelua, pl. *cin-* "hyrax"	ptKal **kɛnɛ:r*	SNil: morphol (SNil n. suff. *-ua*) (lack B pref.)	
kisiilili, pl. *kikisiilili* "hawk"	ptKal **si:rere*	SNil: distrib; morphol (Nil n. pref. *ki-*)	
ututu, pl. *kiututu* "ground hornbill"	Keyo *u:tutu*	SNil: phonol (unusual for B word shape)	
eeeyi, pl. *ci-* "steer"	ptSNil **e:i*	SNil: distrib; phonol (SNil *r* > *φ*)	
euunua, pl. *ci-* "bull"	?	SNil: morphol (SNil n. suff. *-ua*)	
lisisiye, pl. *kama-* "cow dung"	ptSNil **sike* "mud, cow dung"	SNil: distrib; morphol (*-iye* = form of SNil n. suff. *-ia*) (lack B pref.)	pre-Buk. *-*ki-* > Buk. *-si-*

147

BUKUSU	SOUTHERN NILOTIC ATTESTATION	SOURCE	COMMENTS
xabutusi, pl. *ru-* "cow's 'heel'"	ptSNil **pu:tul* "hoof"	SNil: distrib; morphol (lack B pref.)	
-cal- "to bleed cattle"	ptKal **car*	SNil: phonol (*l*)	*l* for SNil **r*
silabina, pl. *bi-* "special arrow for bleeding cattle"	?	SNil: morphol (SNil agent n. suff. *-in*)	
-saac- "to cut up meat"	ptKal **sa:c*	SNil: distrib	
elooyua, pl. *ci-* "capon"	?	SNil: morphol (SNil n. suff. *-ua*)	
-but- "to pluck"	ptKal **put*	SNil: distrib	
-cub- "to take oath"	ptKal **cup*	SNil: distrib	

AGE-SET NAMES:

BUKUSU	SOUTHERN NILOTIC ATTESTATION	SOURCE	COMMENTS
sisaawa, pl. *bi-*	ptKal **sɔ:we* (preSNil **sɔ:e*)	SNil: distrib; morphol (lack B pref)	*a* for SNil **ɔ*
sikolonkolo, pl. *bi-*	ptKal **koronkoro* (preSNil)	SNil: distrib; morphol (lack B pref.)	
sikikwameti, pl. *bi-*	ptKal **kɪpkɔ:ɪmɛt*	SNil distrib; morphol (lack B pref.) (Kal deriv pref. *kɪp-*)	
sikananaci, pl. *bi-*	Kony *kamnɛnɛci*	SNil: morphol (*kam-* = form of Kal deriv pref. *kap-*)	*a* for SNil ɛ
sikinyekeu, pl. *bi-*	ptKal **kimnyekeu*	SNil: distrib; morphol (*kim-* = form of Kal deriv pref. *kip-*)	
sisinyanke, pl. *bibi-*	ptKal **nyɔ:nki* (preSNil)	SNil: distrib; morphol (lack B pref.)	*a* for SNil **ɔ*
simaina, pl. *bi-*	ptKal **maina* (preSNil)	SNil: distrib; morphol (lack B pref.)	
sicuuma, pl. *bi-*	ptKal **cu:ma* (preSNil)	SNil: distrib; morphol (lack B pref.)	

Bukusu	Southern Nilotic Attestation	Source	Comments
-rany- "to forge iron"	ptSNil **ta:ny* "to forge iron"	SNil: distrib	*r* for SNil **t*
mwiranyi, pl. *babeeranyi* "blacksmith"			
eoocua, pl. *ci-* "leather sack"	?	SNil: morphol (SNil n. suff. *-ua*)	
sikolonco, pl. *bi-* "potsherd"	?	SNil: morphol (*-co* = form of SNil n. suff. *-io* after *n-*)	
litooce, pl. *kama-* "partition"	ptKal **to:t*	SNil: distrib; morphol (lack B pref.)	*c* for SNil *t* (before front vowel?)
-maal- "to plaster"	ptKal **ma:l*	SNil: distrib	
-seer- "to raid"	ptKal **sɛ:t*	SNil: distrib	*r* for SNil **t*

D.12

Dadog Loanwords in Sonjo

SONJO	DADOG ATTESTATION	SOURCE
ngai "giraffe"	*qæid*	Dadog: phonol (*q*)
buray, pl. *maray* "jackal"	*fura:yo:d*	Dadog: phonol (*f*)
ndaraweti "impala"	*dæræwe:d*; ptSNil **terɛwe:t*	SNil: distrib; morphol (lack B pref.). Dadog: specif. shape (*d* for SNil **t*, *a* for SNil **ɛ*; Kal **terɛwe:t* would > *ntɛrɛwet-* in Sonjo)
sɛɛm "calf fold"	*sæhæmo:d* "milk-cow fold"	Dadog: phonol (*h*)
mwalit, pl. *meelit* "cattle fold"	*mo:hæ:le:d*	Dadog: phonol (*h*); morphol (SNil sec. suff. in *t*)
-sakat- "to hunt"	*šægæ:d*; ptSNil **lʸɔkɔ:t*	SNil: distrib. Dadog: specif. shape (Sonjo *s* for Dadog *š* < ptSNil **lʸ*)
sankaayɛk "woman's earring"	*sæ:ngæ:nd*, pl. *sæ:ngæ:yo:jig*	Dadog: morphol (SNil pl. sec. suff. in *k*)
horik "stool"	*ho:rgi:d*	?

VOCABULARY SOURCES:
    (1)   *Sonjo:* see Appendix D.7.
    (2)   *Dadog:* see Appendix B.1.

Dadog Loanwords in Nyaturu

NYATURU	DADOG ATTESTATION	SOURCE	COMMENTS
digida "donkey"	*dige:d*	Dadog: morphol (SNil sec. suff. in *t*)	
+*ŋwadida* "lion"		Dadog: morphol (SNil sec suff. in *t*)	
+*mwadida* nickname for war leader	*ŋadi:d*		
+*lughumida* "hide finger ring"	*lu:gme:d*	Dadog: morphol (SNil sec. suff. in *t*)	
+*sumanda* "cave under kraal"	*šo:ma:nd* "cave"	Dadog: morphol (SNil sec. suff. in *t*); phonol (*š*)	
+*msalahuka* "female twin"	*sælæ:ho:g* "twin"	Dadog: morphol (SNil pl. sec. suff. in *k*) (lack B pref.)	
siuli "white cow"	Dadog *si:wo:ld* "eland"	Dadog: phonol (not usual B shape); deriv	Semantics: common East African: cf. Masai -*sirua* "eland; white (cow)"
muli "dark red cow"	Dadog **mur* "tawny" (ptSNil **mur-* "brown")	SNil: distrib; phonol (*r*)	
seneku "dark cow, with spotted tail"	Dadog *sæ:næ:ku*	Dadog: phonol (*æ*)	
buasi "dappled black-and-white cow"	Dadog -*ba:š* or -*bua:š*	Dadog: phonol (*š*)	

Nyaturu	Dadog Attestation	Source	Comments
isamu "gray cow, dark-spotted"	Dadog *sa:mu* (ptSNil **sa:mu-*)	SNil: distrib	

VOCABULARY SOURCES:

(1) *Nyaturu:* Words preceded by a plus (+) were supplied by Marguerite Jellicoe; the word without a plus is from Howard Olson, "Spoken Rimi (Nyaturu)" (unpublished), a work also graciously made available to the writer by Marguerite Jellicoe.

(2) *Dadog:* see Appendix B.1.

D.14

Kalenjin Loanwords in Gusii

Gusii	Kalenjin Attestation	Source	Comments
ɛrɔɔri, pl. *ci-* "heifer"	ptKal **rɔːr-*	Kal: distrib; morphol (lack B pref.)	
emingici, pl. *ci-* "ram"	ptKal **meːnkic*	Kal: distrib; morphol (lack B pref.)	
ɛngɛtia, pl. *cin-* "testicle"	Nandi *ketio*	Kal: morphol (SNil n. suff. -*ia*) (lack B pref.)	*g* for Kal *k
eguutɔ, pl. *ci-* "aardvark"	ptN **kuːto*	Kal: morphol (lack B pref.)	*g* for Kal *k
ekenyinyi, pl. *ebinyinyi* "leech"	ptKal **pinyiny*	Kal: distrib	Kal *pi-* interpreted as B pl. n. pref. *bi-*
rigomia, pl. *ama-* "banana"	ptN **mokoːmia*	Kal: morphol (SNil n. suff. -*ia*)	*g* for Kal *k
ɔrɔgiɔ, pl. *cindɔgiɔ* "potsherd"	Nandi *rokco* (< *rokio)	Kal: morphol (SNil n. suff. -*iɔ*)	*g for* Kal *k
etooto, pl. *ci-* "partition"	ptKal **toːt-*	Kal: distrib; morphol (lack B pref.)	
eanga, pl. *ci-* "cloth"	ptKal **anka*	Kal: distrib; morphol (lack B pref.)	
eguutua, pl. *ci-* a kind of headdress	Nandi *kutua* any headdress	Kal: morphol (SNil n. suff. -*ua*) (lack B pref.)	*g* for Kal *k
-tiɛn- "to play"	ptKal **tɪɛn* "to dance"	Kal: distrib	

ORIGIN: A Kalenjin dialect, probably Nandian. Reason: several of the words occur only in Nandian, but none occurs exclusively in one of the other Kalenjin dialect groups. Time of borrowing: since the end of the proto-Kalenjin period, perhaps in the proto-Nandian period or later.

VOCABULARY SOURCES:
    (1)   *Gusii:* see Appendix D.1.
    (2)   Kalenjin: see Appendix B.1.

D.15

Sonjo Word-sharings with East Kalenjin

East Kalenjin Attestation	Sonjo Attestation	Source
Kam. *mbutwoi* "woman's breast"	*mbuduai* "chest"	?
Kam. *enturume* "ram"	*ndurum*; but cf. cognate Buk. *enturume* "he-goat," Kikuyu *ndorome* "ram"	Bantu: distrib; morphol (B pref.)
Tind. *kiret* "pot"	*lukɛr*, pl. *n-*	Kal: morphol (lack B pref.)

ORIGIN: Heterogeneous; the items have been put together for convenience; discrimination and interpretation will require much better evidence from the Dorobo dialects.

VOCABULARY SOURCES:
    (1)   East Kalenjin: see Appendix B.1.
    (2)   *Sonjo:* see Appendix D.7.

Appendixes E.1–E.6

Bantu Loanword Sets in Southern Nilotic

E.1

Bantu Loanwords in Pre– and Proto–Southern Nilotic

Southern Nilotic	Bantu Attestation	Source	Comments
ptKal *moi:ŋ(k)- (preSNil *mori:ŋ(k)-) "beehive"	Eastn Bantu *(mu)rînga	Bantu: distrib; morphol (B pref. mu-)	o for B *u
Dadog mbo:id (preSNil *mbo:ri-) "goat"	ptB *-burî	Bantu: distrib; morphol (B pref. m-)	o for B *u
ptSNil *ɪsɪɔ- "mano"	EVicB *isio	Bantu: deriv (< B "to grind"); morphol (B pref. i-)	

Origin: Undetermined Bantu language. Time of borrowing: before end of late pre–Southern Nilotic period, because preSNil r is lost.

Vocabulary sources:
    (1)   Southern Nilotic: see Appendix B.1.
    (2)   Bantu: see Appendix D.1.

Bantu Loanwords in Proto-Kalenjin

PROTO-KALENJIN	BANTU ATTESTATION	SOURCE	COMMENTS
*pʊsia "flour"	EVicB *busie	Bantu: deriv (B "to grind"); morphol (B pref. bu-)	ʊ for B *u
*mu:ser "gruel"	Buk. busela, Id. busala or busela, Jita obusara	Bantu: morphol (B pref. mu-)	u for B *u; r for B *l; mu for B pref. bu-
*mʊka:ŋ(k)- "large spoon"	EVicB *-ganga	Bantu: morphol (B pref. mu-)	ʊ for B *u
*maka:nta "beans"	Luhyia-Gishu *makanda	Bantu: morphol (B pref. ma-)	
*sɛ:mpɛr "to weed"	Luhyia *-sembel-	Bantu: phonol (mb typical B, rare SNil); morphol (B v. ext. -el-)	
*musuk "tree stump"	ptB *-siki	Bantu: morphol (B pref. mu-)	u for B *u; mu for B pref. *ki-
*mu:sa:mpwa:n "(evil) spirit"	EVic and Uganda B *musambwa	Bantu: morphol (B pref. mu-)	u for B *u

ORIGIN: An East Victoria Bantu language. Reason: a number of the items occur only in East Victoria languages. Time of borrowing: before the end of the proto-Kalenjin period but probably after the close of the proto–Southern Nilotic times because the loanwords of that era (Appendix E.1) have o instead of u for Bantu *u.

COMPARISON: Source language is probably the same language as the source of the loanwords of Appendix E.3. Reason: same phonetic features, r for Bantu *l and u or ʊ for Bantu *u.

VOCABULARY SOURCES:
    (1)   Kalenjin: see Appendix B.1.
    (2)   Bantu: see Appendix D.1.

Bantu Loanwords in Kony

KONY	BANTU ATTESTATION	SOURCE	COMMENTS
rwa:ntɛt "stone"	Luhyia-Gishu *(lu)anda	Bantu: morphol (B pref. ru-)	r for B *l; u(w) for B *u
rʌkɔnkait (< *rʊkɔ:nkɔ-) "district"	Gusii ɔrɔgɔngɔ	Bantu: morphol (B pref. ru-)	r for Gusii r (B *l); ʊ for B *u
mʌsinɛt (< *mʊsi:na) "lower tree trunk"	ptB *-tîna	Bantu: distrib; morphol (B pref. mu-)	ʊ for B *u; mu- for usual B pref. *ki-; si for B *tî
mʌtarakwɛt "juniper"	Cf. Buk. kumutarakwe	Bantu: morphol (B pref. mu- = mʌ-)	ʊ for B *u; mu- where Buk. has kumu-
kasʌrya:ntɛt "small weeding hoe"	Buk. sisili, Id. xixili	Bantu: morphol (B pref. ka-)	ka- for Luhyia-Gishu *ki pref.
makonkɛt "iron hoe"	?	Bantu: morphol (B pref. ma-)	
makorɨk "banana bark"	Luhyia-Gishu *-kola	Bantu: morphol (B pref. ma-)	r for B *l
mašekek "unsieved beer"	?	Bantu: morphol (B pref. ma-)	
marɔrya:ntɛt "grass for fermenting banana beer"	?	Bantu: morphol (B pref. ma-)	r for presumed B *l
kɨpa:nkayit "very big pot"	Buk. sipanka	Bantu: morphol (B pref. ki-)	ki for Buk. si-
ma:ka:nkɛt "guinea fowl"	ptB *-kanga; Buk. kamakanka (pl.)	Bantu: distrib; morphol (B pref. ma-)	ma- where Buk. has kama-
ntotya:ntɛt "banana"	Buk. litoore (< *-toote)	Bantu: morphol (B pref. n-)	n- for Buk. li- pref.

Kony	Bantu Attestation	Source	Comments
matumwɛt "ensete"	?	Bantu: morphol (B pref. *ma-*)	
ruta:yit "beer-straw sheath"	Buk. *litaya*	Bantu: morphol (B pref. *ru-*)	*r* for B *l*; *ru* for Buk. *li-* pref.
mʌsa:nkoinɛk "sacrifice"	Luhyia-Gishu *(mu)sango*	Bantu: morphol (B pref. *mu-*); deriv (< B "to sacrifice")	u for B *u*

ORIGIN: An East Victoria Bantu language, closest to modern Luhyia and Gishu dialects, but not identifiable with any modern language. Reason: attestation of the words is often limited only to East Victoria languages, more often only to Luhyia-Gishu; but in the source language the words show special morphological (prefix) and phonological developments not shared with other East Victoria languages; also some of the words, while clearly of Bantu source, are not attested in present-day Bantu languages.

COMPARISON: See Appendix E.2.

SPECIAL POINTS: See Appendix G.1, "Special points" (1).

VOCABULARY SOURCES:
    (1) *Kony:* see Appendix B.1.
    (2) Bantu: see Appendix D.1.

E.4

Bantu Loanwords in Nandian

Nandian	Bantu Attestation	Source	Comments
ptNd *moko:mpe "hoe"	Gusii obokombe, Kuria omokombe, Ganda omukumbi	Bantu: morphol (B pref. mo-)	o for B *u; e for B *i
ptNd *moko:mia, pl. *moko:m "banana tree"	Gusii rigoma "ensete"	Bantu: morphol (B pref. mo-)	o for B *u; mo- for B pref. ri-
Nandi mototia, pl. motot "banana"	Bukusu ritoore (< *-toote)	Bantu: morphol (B pref. mo-)	o for B *u; mo- for B pref. ri-
ptNd *rokor "beer straw"	Gusii orokore	Bantu: morphol (B pref. ro-)	o for B *u
Nandi kitonga "basket"	Gusii ɛgɛtɔnga	Bantu: morphol (B pref. ki-)	ki- for B ki-
Nandi nianja "lake"	ptB *nyanja; ptEVicB *nyanja	Bantu: distrib; morphol (B pref. ny-)	

ORIGIN: Probably Gusii dialect. Reasons: (1) most of the words are attested in Gusii or only in Gusii; (2) o for Bantu *u as in Gusii. Time of borrowing: before the end of the proto-Nandian period but since the end of the proto-Kalenjin period, because Bantu loans in proto-Kalenjin have u instead of o for Bantu *u.

VOCABULARY SOURCES:

 (1) Proto-Nandian vocabulary items were reconstructed on the basis of word materials collected for *Tuken*, *Keyo*, and *Nandi*. See Appendix B.1.
 (2) Bantu: see Appendix D.1.

Bantu Loanwords in Akie

AKIE	BANTU ATTESTATION	SOURCE	COMMENTS
mataki: "egg"	Zigula, Shambala, Bondei *matagi* "eggs"	Bantu: morphol (B pref. *ma-*); deriv (< B "to lay eggs")	
mantolo:i "potato, yam"	Luguru *mandolo*	Bantu: morphol (lack final Akie vowel)	*l* for B **l*
mpeyui "seed"	Widespread EastnB **-beyu* (Zigula *mbeyu*)	Bantu: distrib; morphol (B pref. *m-*)	*u* for B **u*
mpokai "vegetable"	ptB **-boga* (Zigula *mboga*)	Bantu: distrib; morphol (B pref. *m-*)	
ʊnka:i "flour"	EastnB **-yunga* (Zigula *unga*)	Bantu: distrib	ʊ for B **u*
mutinko: "large spoon"	Common central Tanz. B **-tinko* (not in Zigula)	Bantu: morphol (B pref. *mu-*)	*u* for B **u*
ku:nku:rue: "crow"	EastnB **-kunguulu* (Zigula *kungulu*)	Bantu: distrib; morphol (lack Akie suff. = form of SNil *-ua*)	*r* for B **l*
kɪsɛkɛ "basket"	Zigula *sege*	Bantu: phonol (*g*); morphol (B pref. *ki-*)	

ORIGIN: A Bantu dialect or Bantu dialects closely related to those spoken today along the east and southeast of the Masai steppe. Reason: several words are limited in distribution to that area. Time of borrowing: since the end of the proto-Kalenjin period.

VOCABULARY SOURCES:
Akie: see Appendix B.1.

E.6

Bantu Loanwords in Dadog

Dadog	Bantu Attestation	Source	Comments
bu:la:li:d "bed"	ptB *-laal-* "to sleep"	Bantu: morphol (B pref. *bu-*); deriv (< B "to sleep")	*u* for B *u*
mage:mnyæ:nd, pl. *mage:mo:jig* "iron hoe"	Widespread EastnB *-gembe*	Bantu: morphol (B pref. *ma-*)	
ma:di:ngo:d "large wooden spoon"	Common central and eastn Tanz. B *-tinko*	Bantu: morphol (B pref. *ma-*)	
ma:dæ:ndajæ:nd "dried meat"	Widespread Kenya and Tanz. B *-tande, -tanda* (< ptB *-tand-* "to spread out"); cf. Swahili *mtande*	Bantu: distrib; morphol (B pref. *ma-*); deriv	
ma:rgwe:g "millet beer"	Widespread Southern and EastnB *-alua*	Bantu: distrib; morphol (B pref. *ma-*)	Dadog C*gw-* < *C*w-*

ORIGIN: Undetermined Bantu language; not language of loanwords of Appendix E.1. Reason: *u* for Bantu *u* instead of *o*.

VOCABULARY SOURCES:
   Dadog: see Appendix B.1.

162

Appendixes F.1–F.4

Southern Nilotic Loanword Sets in Eastern Nilotic

Southern Nilotic Loanwords in Proto–Teso-Masaian

Proto–Teso-Masaian	Southern Nilotic Attestation	Source	Comments
*-osowuan "buffalo"	ptKal *sɔ:(i)- (preSNil *sɔ:ri-)	SNil: distrib; phonol (loss of r is SNil change); morphol (form of SNil n. suff. -ua)	Lacks preSNil *r; o for SNil *ɔ
*-ŋatuny "lion"	ptSNil *ŋet(uny)	SNil: morphol (SNil n. suff. in ny, now unprodc)	a for SNil *e; see H.1, "lion"
*-sikiria "donkey"	ptKal *sɪkɪrɪɔ	SNil: morphol (SNil n. suff. -ia)	ia for Kal -ɪɔ
*-mɔrɔk "spear haft"	Dadog mo:ro:gu:d	SNil: morphol (lack TMas pref.)	
*-(k)ameu "dry season"	ptKal *kemeu "hunger; dry season"	SNil: morphol (lack TMas pref.); deriv (see B.20)	1st syllable a for SNil e as in "lion"
*-pʊs "bluish-gray (cow)"	ptSNil *pu:sie:n-	?	
Teso akol "white-patched (cow)"	Dadog -qo:l	SNil: phonol (q)	
Turkana manaŋit, pl. ŋemanaŋ "small calf"	ptSNil *mɪnɪŋ "small"	SNil: distrib; morphol (lack KT affixes); deriv (< SNil adj.)	a for SNil ɪ; see H.1, "small"
Lotuko atɔgɔl "beehive"	ptSNil *toqol "honey container"	SNil: distrib; phonol (q); morphol (lack TMas pref.)	

ORIGIN: Descendant language of proto–Southern Nilotic. Reason: preSNil r lost in proto–Southern Nilotic is lacking in one word ("buffalo"). Time of borrowing: since proto–Southern Nilotic times because of loss of preSNil r in "buffalo." Southern Nilotic loanwords limited to one of the Teso-Masaian languages (cf. last three entries) are so few as to be most probably original proto–Teso-Masaian borrowings by chance lost in the other Teso-Masaian languages.

COMPARISON: Source language possibly closely related to source of loanwords of Appendix
H.1. Reason: same shape for words "lion" and "small" as in that appendix.

VOCABULARY SOURCES:

Proto–Teso-Masaian reconstructions are tentative and based on comparison of vocabularies of *Masai* and *Ongamo* (see F.3 and F.4, respectively, for sources of these vocabularies) with Karamojong-Teso vocabularies from the following sources:

Teso: J. H. Hilders and J. C. D. Lawrence, *An English-Ateso and Ateso-English Vocabulary* (Kampala: Eagle Press, 1958), and Lawrence, *The Iteso* (London: Oxford University Press, 1957).

Turkana: Juxon Barton, "Turkana Grammatical Notes and Vocabulary," *Bulletin of the School of Oriental and African Studies*, II (1921), 43–73.

Lotuko: C. Muratori, *English-Bari-Lotuxo-Acoli Vocabulary* (Okaru: Catholic Mission Printing Press, 1948).

Southern Nilotic Loanwords in Proto-Masaian

Proto-Masaian	Southern Nilotic Attestation	Source	Comments
*-ɪnkatu "wildebeest"	ptSNil *ɪnqat	SNil: distrib; phonol (q); morphol (lack Mas pref.)	
*-sirua "eland; eland-colored cow"	ptKal *si:rua "eland-colored cow"	SNil: morphol (SNil n. suff. -ua)	
*-motonyi "vulture"	ptSNil *moto:ny	SNil: distrib; morphol (SNil n. suff. in ny, now unprodc) (lack Mas pref.)	
*-(k)olupa "centipede, scorpion"	Dadog o:lu:bdo:d "centipede"	SNil: morphol (lack Mas pref.)	
*-caɲito "wild animal"	ptSNil *tiɔ:ny (preSNil)	SNil: distrib; morphol (SNil sec. suff. in t) (SNil n. suff. in ny? now unprodc) (lack Mas pref.)	a for SNil ɔ
*-supeni "young ewe"	ptKal *supe:n (preSNil)	SNil: distrib; morphol (lack Mas pref.)	
*-tarakuai "juniper"	ptKal *tarakua	SNil: morphol (SNil n. suff. -ua) (lack Mas pref.)	
*-lɔŋɔ, pl. -loŋoi "shield"	ptSNil *lɔ:ŋ-	SNil: distrib; morphol (lack Mas pref.)	
*-mʊrrani "young circumcised man"	ptKal *muren (preSNil *mura)	SNil: distrib; morphol (SNil n. suff. -n) (lack Mas pref.)	a for SNil *e
*-mʊrat "to circumcise"	ptKal *mʊra:tan (preSNil)	SNil: distrib; deriv (< stem *mur in *muren, Nandi murmur "to cut in small pieces," etc.)	

Possible Members of This Loanword Set Attested Today Only in Masai

PROTO-MASAIAN	SOUTHERN NILOTIC ATTESTATION	SOURCE	COMMENTS
Masai ɛ-sʊnyai, pl. ɪ-sʊnya "fat piece of meat"	ptKal *su:nɛ:t	SNil: morphol (-ya = form of SNil n. suff. -ia)	
Masai ol-teani "bamboo"	ptSNil *te:q(ia:n)	SNil: morphol (SNil n. suff. -an)	
Masai o-lenyua "fly-whisk"	?	SNil: morphol (SNil n. suff. -ua)	
Masai -mɪšɪr "to brand"	ptSNil *mece:i- (preSNil *mece:ri-)	SNil: distrib	preSNil r retained
Masai e-sekekua "wooden horn"	?	SNil: morphol (SNil n. suff. -ua)	

ORIGIN: Pre–Southern Nilotic language. Reasons: see Chapter 4. Time of borrowing: see Chapter 4.

SPECIAL POINTS: The last five entries are suggested as possible members of the set because they are not attributable, either by shape or through lack of attestation, to either Kalenjin or Dadog, although they appear to be from a Southern Nilotic language.

VOCABULARY SOURCES:
(1) Proto-Masaian forms were based on vocabulary materials collected for *Masai* and *Ongamo*. For respective sources of these materials see Appendixes F.3 and F.4.
(2) Southern Nilotic: see Appendix B.1.

Kalenjin Loanwords in Masai

Masai	Kalenjin Attestation	Source	Comments
ol-kirisiet "hammer"	ptKal **kiri:sua*; Akie *kirisie:*	Kal: morphol (form of SNil n. suff. *-ia*) (SNil sec. suff. in *t*). SKal: specif. shape	
en-tereet "pot"	ptKal **ter*	Kal: morphol (SNil sec. suff. in *t*) (lack Mas pref.)	
ɛn-taritiki, pl. *ɛn-taritik* "small bird"	ptSNil **tari:t*, ptKal **tari:t* "bird"	SNil: morphol (SNil pl. sec. suff. in *t*) (lack Mas pref.)	
ol-meeki, pl. *il-meek* "agriculturist"	ptKal **me:(i)-* "person without property in cattle; agriculturist"	Kal: morphol (SNil pl. sec. suff. in *k*) (lack Mas pref.)	
+*ol-kerenget* "pit trap"	ptKal **keri:nko* "deep pit, pit trap"	Kal: morphol (SNil sec. suff. in *t*) (lack Mas pref.)	
o-sosian "stick for cleaning calabashes"	ptKal **so:siɔ(:n)*	Kal: morphol (SNil n. suff. *-ian*) (lack Mas pref.)	*-ian* for Kal **-iɔ(:n)*
ɔl-payian "elder"	ptKal **pɔ:iyɔ(:n)*	Kal: morphol (SNil n. suff. *-ian*) (lack Mas pref.)	*-ian* for Kal **-iɔ(:n)*
o-suyiani "wild dog"	ptSNil **su:iyɔ(:n)*, ptKal **su:iyɔ(:n)*	SNil: morphol (SNil n. suff. *-ian*) (lack Mas pref.)	*-ian* for Kal **-iɔ(:n)*
ɛ-mɔɔtian "quiver"	ptKal **mɔ:t-*	Kal: morphol (SNil n. suff. *-ian*) (lack Mas pref.)	
ɛn-tamɪs "camel"	ptKal **tɔm(p)ɛs*	Kal: morphol (lack Mas pref.)	*a* for Kal **ɔ*
ɛ-sampʊr "pouch"	ptKal **sɔ:mpʊr* "a kind of hide sack"	Kal: morphol (lack Mas pref.)	*a* for Kal **ɔ*

MASAI	KALENJIN ATTESTATION	SOURCE	COMMENTS
ɛnk-anyɪt "honor"	ptKal *kɔ:nyit	Kal: morphol (lack Mas pref.)	a for Kal *ɔ
ɔl-mʊrʊnya "razor"	Nandi murunyo	Kal: morphol (lack Mas pref.)	a for presumed Kal *ɔ
+ɔl-karia "red ochre"	Nandi ŋario	Kal: morphol (SNil n. suff. -ia) (lack Mas pref.)	a for presumed Kal *ɔ; k for Nandi ŋ
ɔŋata/aŋata "plains"	Nandi oŋata	?	
en-terit "dust"	ptKal *te:ri:t	Kal: morphol (SNil n. suff. t, now unprodc) (lack Mas pref.)	
ɛ-matua "half"	Nandi matua	Kal: morphol (SNil n. suff. -ua) (lack Mas pref.)	
ɛ-sanca "lover"	ptKal *sa:n- (preSNil *sa:n- "friend")	SNil: distrib; morphol (-ca is form of SNil n. suff. -ia) (lack Mas pref.). Kal: specif. meaning	
ol-porror "age set"	ptKal *poror, Nandi meaning = "large warrior band," Pokot = "people of one's district," Akie = "age set"	Kal: distrib; morphol (lack Mas pref.)	Akie meaning same as Masai, but perhaps because of recent Masai influence
e-sirit "age-set band"	Nandi sirit	Kal: morphol (lack Mas pref.)	
a-sakut "to bewitch"	ptKal *sa:kut- or *sa:kit- "medicine"; Kony sekut- "to bewitch cattle"; Nandi sakutin, pl. sakut "evil eye"	Kal: distrib; deriv (< original stem *sa:k- seen also in Nandi sakeyuo "medicine man")	Nandi -in/φ forms agent n. < v.; so "evil eye" = "bewitcher"? < v. "to bewitch"

MASAI	KALENJIN ATTESTATION	SOURCE	COMMENTS
ɛ-sɛtan "witchcraft"	ptKal *sɛ:tan "amulet"	Kal: morphol (SNil n. suff. -an) (lack Mas pref.)	
ɔl-kɛsɛn "baby sling"	ptKal *kɛsɛn "to carry baby, load"	Kal: distrib; deriv (< Kal v. of more general meaning)	
en-kupes "thigh"	ptSNil *kupe:s, ptKal *kupe:s	SNil: distrib; morphol (SNil n. suff. -s)	
+ɔl-maranguš a kind of headdress	Nandi kimaranguc	Kal: morphol (lack Mas pref.). Not Nandi: specif. shape	
en-kuyukui "puppy"	Pokot ku:kwi:ɣ "dog"; cf. Keyo cukui "dog" < earlier *kyukui ?	Kal: morphol (lack Mas pref.)	
aros, pl. ink-arusi "black-white spotted, on underbody"	ptKal *a:ru:s/*ɔ:ru:s, Nandi meaning = "blue," Pokot = "gray," Kony = "black, with gray head"	Kal: distrib	For meaning confusion cf. also Kal *pu:siɛ(:n); sometimes = "blue, gray," other times "spotted"; two words at one time became confused in usage
keri "having black stomach, white back"	Kony keri "having white stomach, black back"	?	
ɔl-mɔɔikɪ, pl. ɪl-mɔɔikɪn "steer calf"	ptSNil *mɔ:i-, ptKal *mɔ:i- "calf"	SNil: distrib; morphol (SNil pl. sec. suff. in k) (lack Mas pref.)	
ɔl-tatuani, pl. ɪl-tatua "an Iraqw, an Mbugwe"	Cf. Dadog dado:g (< *tat-) "the Dadog"	SNil: morphol (SNil n. suff. -ua) (lack Mas pref.)	For semantics see Chap. 7

170

ORIGIN: A South Kalenjin dialect. Reasons: (1) phonological developments limited to South Kalenjin (*a* for ptKal *ɔ); (2) South Kalenjin morphological development: *-ia:n* for proto-Kalenjin suffix **-iɔ*(*:n*); (3) specific shape similarity (hammer) of Masai and South Kalenjin forms of a word. Time of borrowing: since the end of the proto-Kalenjin period.

VOCABULARY SOURCES:

(1) *Masai:* Stanley Ole Mukishae, about 25 to 30 years old, of the Kaputie tribe, from Mashuru; and John Ole Sailenyi, about the same age, of the Purko tribe, from Bissil, near Kajiado, Kenya. Entries preceded by a plus (+) are taken from Johannes Hohenberger, *Semitisches und hamitisches Sprachgut im Masai* (Sachsenmühle: Privately printed, 1958). Also consulted was A. N. Tucker and John Tompo Ole Mpaayei, *A Masai Grammar* (London: Longmans, 1955).

(2) Kalenjin: see Appendix B.1.

Southern Nilotic Loanwords in Ongamo

Ongamo	Southern Nilotic Attestation	Source	Comments
nasuii "wild dog"	ptSNil *su:i-*, sing. *su:iyɔ(:n)*	SNil: distrib; morphol (lack Ongamo pref.)	
naseleβai "cockroach"	ptKal *solop-*	SNil: distrib; morphol (lack Ongamo pref.)	Ongamo *e* for SNil *o*
namakata "sheepskin"	ptKal *makata*	SNil: distrib; morphol (lack Ongamo pref.)	
-βar "to cultivate"	ptSNil *par*	SNil: distrib	
naβurɔi "arrow poison"	Dadog *furo:d*	SNil: phonol (*f*); morphol (lack Ongamo pref.)	
nasɪkɛtɔ a kind of spoon	ptNd *se:ke:t*	SNil: morphol (lack Ongamo pref.)	
namɔngɛ "cap of colobus monkey skin"	ptKal *-mɔ:nkɛ:s* "colobus monkey"	SNil: distrib; morphol (lack Ongamo pref.)	
nipani "honeycomb"	ptKal *po:not* "natural hive"	SNil: morphol (lack Ongamo pref.)	Ongamo *a* for SNil *o*
ohoriu "homestead"	ptSNil *qo:r-* "homesteads"	SNil: distrib; morphol (lack Ongamo pref.)	Ongamo *h* < *k*
narakati a kind of basket	ptSNil *(y)a:ra:k-* "a container"	SNil: distrib; morphol (SNil sec. suff. in *t*) (lack Ongamo pref.)	

ORIGIN: Probably pre–Southern Nilotic language; not late Kalenjin or Dadog. Reason: many of the words have significant phonological or morphological differences from either Kalenjin, Dadog, or proto–Southern Nilotic forms of the words. Some individual words, however, might be of later Kalenjin derivation, e.g., "sheepskin"; an individual word or two may also be later from Dadog, like "poison."

VOCABULARY SOURCES:
(1) *Ongamo:* Petre Mutui, about 60 years old, and Kahumba, more than 70 years old, both of Reha (Kilimanjaro), Tanzania.
(2) Southern Nilotic: see Appendix B.1.

Appendixes G.1–G.3

Eastern Nilotic Loanword Sets
in Southern Nilotic

G.1

Karamojong-Teso Loanwords in Pokot

POKOT	KARAMOJONG-TESO ATTESTATION	SOURCE	COMMENTS
a:ra:ra: "cheetah"	ptKT *-rara*	KT: morphol (KT n. pref. *a-*)	
adɨr "oryx"	ptKT *-dir*	KT: phonol (*d*); morphol (KT pref.)	
aluru "quail"	ptKT *aluru*	KT: morphol (KT pref.)	
lodiryo "kind of sunbird"	?	KT: morphol (KT pref. *lo-*)	
amʌrʌtot "python"	ptKT *amorotot-*	KT: morphol (KT pref.)	
a:na:m "lake"	ptKT *-nam*	KT: morphol (KT pref.)	
akadɨlwa:y a kind of plant	?	KT: phonol (*d*); morphol (KT pref.)	
otupɔ "wooden basin"	ptKT *-tuba*	KT: morphol (KT n. pref. *o-*)	
a:teker "watering trough"	ptKT *-teker*	KT: morphol (KT pref.)	
akɔkɔrɔy "chicken"	ptKT *-kɔkɔrɔ*	KT: morphol (KT pref.)	ptTMas ?: cf. Lotuko *axɔxɔrɔ*
ameleko "iron hoe"	ptKT *-meleko*	KT: morphol (KT pref.)	
ama:yde "groundnut"	Teso *emaido*	KT: phonol (*d*); morphol (KT pref.)	
aperɨt "outside sleeping place for children"	ptKT *-pɛr-* "to lie down, sleep"	KT: morphol (KT pref.); deriv (< KT verb)	
apedon "woman's large earring"	?	KT: morphol (KT pref.)	
a:telʌ "girl's apron"	?	KT: morpohl (KT pref.)	

ORIGIN: A Karamojong-Teso dialect very closely related to the modern dialects.

SPECIAL POINTS: (1) Pokot *o*, *u*, *e*, *i*, *ɔ*, ʊ, *ε*, and ɪ have elsewhere been written *o:*, *u:*, etc. But such explicit representation of these vowels as long is unnecessary since in Pokot they occur only long. Only for Pokot *a:* and *a* is there a phonemic vowel-length distinction. The same comments generally hold also for Kony; see Appendix E.3.
(2) The loanword set above is just a small sample of the great number of Karamojong-Teso loanwords in Pokot. A small sample seemed sufficient because the presence of Karamojong-Teso loanwords in Pokot is generally accepted.

VOCABULARY SOURCES:
(1) *Pokot:* see Appendix B.1.
(2) Karamojong-Teso: see Appendix F.1.

G.2

Masaian Loanwords in East Kalenjin

East Kalenjin	Masaian Attestation	Source
Kam. *esiminjai* "cat"	Masai *ɛ-sɪmɪnja* "serval cat"	Mas: morphol (Mas sing. pref. *ɛ-*); phonol (*j*)
Kam. *oldau* "heart"	Masai *ol-tau*, ptMas **-tau*	Mas: distrib; morphol (Mas sing. pref. *ol-*)
Kam. *ndolu* "ax"	Masai *en-tolu*, ptMas **-tolu*	Mas: distrib; morphol (Mas sing. pref. *en-*)
Kam. *olgine* "sheep"	Masai *ol-kine*, ptMas **-kine*	Mas: distrib; morphol (Mas sing. pref. *ol-*)
Kam. *engare* "water"	Masai *ɛnk-are*, ptMas **-(k)are*	Mas: distrib; morphol (Mas sing. pref. *ɛn-*)
Kam. *oltongor* "bell"	?	Mas: morphol (Mas sing. pref. *ol-*)
Kam. *olodoi* "blood"	?	Mas: morphol (Mas sing. pref. *ol-*)
Kam. *olpukainyeiya* "cowry"	?	Mas: morphol (Mas sing. pref. *ol-*)
Tind. *ulgwenyat* "bird"	Ongamo *ošɛŋi* (< **-keŋ-*); ptTMas **-kwɛny-*	Mas: morphol (Mas sing. pref. *ol- = ul-*)
Tind. *olusait* "hair"	?	Mas: morphol (Mas sing. pref. *ol-*)
Rav. *eldat* "rain"	?	Mas: morphol (Mas pl. pref. *il- = el-*)
Rav. *oloitit* "bone"	Masai *ol-oito*, ptMas **-oito*	Mas: distrib; morphol (Mas sing. pref. *ol-*)
Rav. *ndabit* "palm of hand"	Masai **ɛn-dap*, ptMas **-dapu*	Mas: distrib; morphol (Mas sing. pref. *ɛn-*)
Rav. *lotoro* "bee"	Masai *ol-otoroi*, ptMas **-otoro*	Mas: distrib; morphol (Mas sing. pref. *ol- = l-*)

East Kalenjin	Masaian Attestation	Source
Rav. *ngwenyat* "bird"	See, above, Tind. "bird"	Mas: distrib; morphol (Mas sing. pref. *en-* = *n-*)
Ndoro *olusuwan* "buffalo"	Masai *ol-osowuan*, ptMas **-osowuan*	Mas: distrib; morphol (Mas sing. pref. *ol-*)
Ndoro *elmaot* "giraffe"	Masai *ɔl-mɛʊt*	Mas: morphol (Mas sing. pref. *ɔl-*)
Ndoro *olimwa* "ashes"	?	? Mas: morphol (Mas sing. pref. *ol-*)

ORIGIN: Different Masaian dialects, most closely related to modern Masai (rather than to Ongamo). Reason: most of the loanwords contain the Masai prefix *ol-*, or a version of this prefix, an innovation in Masai, postdating the split of the ancestor dialects of Ongamo and Masai. While many of the words are not demonstrably other than late loans from modern Masai, in each dialect cited there are Masaian loanwords which are not known or are not normally used in modern Masai. Some or all of such words may be loans from a now extinct Masai dialect.

SPECIAL POINTS: For further examples of Masai loanwords in East Kalenjin and for further tentative conclusions on East Kalenjin history see comments under Appendix A.6.

VOCABULARY SOURCES:
(1) East Kalenjin: see Appendix A.6.
(2) Masaian: see Appendixes F.3 and F.4.

Apparent (Nonattested) Masai Loanwords in Akie

AKIE	TESO-MASAIAN ATTESTATION	SOURCE	COMMENTS
ɪnkɪwɛrɛɪ "bulrush millet"		Mas: morphol (Mas pl. n. pref. ɪn-)	
elukukui "sorghum"		Mas: morphol (Mas sing. n. pref. en- = e- before l)	
ɛmʊtʊːɪ "porridge"		Mas: morphol (Mas sing. n. pref. ɛn- = ɛ- before m)	
ɔlaibakai "gruel"		Mas: morphol (Mas sing. n. pref. ɔl-)	
ɪnkamʊrie "beans"	ptTMas *-mar-; Turk. ŋamari	Mas: morphol (Mas pl. n. pref. ɪn-)	
enkituri "mortar"	Ongamo nakihuri (< *-kituri)	Mas: morphol (Mas sing. n. pref. en-)	
ɛmʊtwaːnkoːi "pestle"		Mas: morphol (Mas sing. n. pref. ɛn- = ɛ- before m)	
enkukui "chicken"		Mas: morphol (Mas sing. n. pref. en-)	
enkitoriaːi "ax"	Masai en-tolu, ptTMas *-tolu	TMas: distrib. Mas: morphol (Mas sing. n. pref. en-). Not modern Masai: specific shape (pref. ki-)	
Mosiro orobout pl. oroboutisie "hartebeest"		Mas: morphol (Mas sing. n. pref. ol-, = o- before r)	Mas source ultim < SNil, cf. Dadog roːbæoːd

ORIGIN: Masai dialect, but not the dialect of modern pastoral Masai. Reason: (1) presence of fossilized Masai prefixes in loanwords indicates the dialect was Masai; but (2) the nonattestation of any of the words in modern Masai indicates that another dialect must have been the source. Time of borrowing: since the end of the proto-Kalenjin period and since the end of the proto-Masaian period but before the present Masai population of the area the Akie live in arrived.

VOCABULARY SOURCES:
      (1)   *Akie:* see Appendix B.1.
      (2)   *Ongamo:* see Appendix F.4. (For *Turkana* see Appendix F.1.)

SPECIAL POINTS: Mosiro is Akie, as recorded in R. A. Maguire, "Il-Torobo . . . ," *Journal of the African Society*, XXVII (1928); see Appendix B.2. It is interesting to note that many of the words (those for "bulrush millet," "porridge," "mortar," "pestle," and "chicken") were originally borrowed by Masaian languages from a Bantu language of eastern Kenya or northeast Tanzania and thus betoken Bantu influence on the agriculture of the Masai, who in turn influenced the South Kalenjin in their agricultural practices.

Appendixes H.1–H.4
Miscellaneous Loanword Sets

H.1.

Southern Nilotic Loanwords in Tepeth

TEPETH	SOUTHERN NILOTIC ATTESTATION	SOURCE	COMMENTS
ŋatuny "lion"	ptSNil *ŋet(uny)*	SNil: distrib; morphol (SNil n. suff. in *ny*, now unprodc). Not ENil: lacks ENil pref. Not recent Pokot: wrong tones	*a* for SNil **e*; see F.1, "lion"
ponot "oribi"	ptKal *po:in-* "bushbuck"	SNil: morphol (SNil sec. suff. in *t*)	V for Kal **Vi*; cf. H.2, "oribi"
nyɛmut "bush duiker"	ptKal *ŋɛmwuɔ*	SNil: morphol (SNil sec. suff. in *t*)	*u* for SNil *-ua*, *-uɔ*; *ny* for Kal *ŋ*
kukut "crocodile"	ptKal *kuikui-*	SNil: morphol (SNil sec. suff. in *t*)	V for Kal **Vi*
nyɛrɛtan, pl. *nyɛrɛtut* "chameleon"	ptKal *nyɪ:rɪ:t*	SNil: morphol (lack Tep. suff. *-an*)	
motony "vulture"	ptSNil *moto(:ny)*	SNil: distrib; morphol (SNil n. suff. in *ny*, now unprodc)	
yukut, pl. *yukutut* "owl"	ptKal *yu:ku:k*	?	*k > t* by dissimil?
tawe, pl. *tawerut* "termite"	ptKal *tɔ:i-*	?	*a* for Kal **ɔ*
tulan, pl. *tuli* "anthill"	ptSNil *tulua* (stem **tul-*)	SNil: distrib.	
lɔt "to castrate"	ptKal *la:t*	SNil: pattern (*ɔ* for Kal **a*, as in "to sew")	*ɔ* for SNil **a*
ipat "field"	ptKal *ipat* "to cultivate"	SNil: morphol (SNil v. caus. pref. *i-*?)	
sikɛt, pl. *sikɛtut* "beer straw"	ptKal *sek-* (preSNil **seke*)	SNil: distrib; morphol (SNil sec. suff. in *t*)	*i* for SNil **e*

Tepeth	Southern Nilotic Attestation	Source	Comments
tɔkɔl, pl. *tokol* "sack"	ptSNil **toqol* "honey sack"	SNil: distrib; phonol (*q*)	
nɔb "to sew"	ptSNil **na:p*	SNil: distrib	*ɔ* for SNil **a*
seitek "needle"	ptSNil **sʌtek-*	SNil: distrib	
kɛny "year"	ptSNil **k(w)ɛ(ny)-*; ptKal **kɛny*	SNil: distrib	
uran, pl. *uri* "shadow"	ptKal **u:r-*	SNil: morphol (lack Tep. n. suff. *-an*)	
manaŋ "small"	ptSNil **mɪnɪŋ*	SNil: distrib	See F.1, "small calf"
lakwan, pl. *lɛkwɛ* "child"	ptKal **lakwa*	SNil: morphol (lack Tep. n. suff. *-an*)	
nyiki "heavy"	ptKal **nyi:k-*	?	
tɛkɛt "chest"	ptSNil **tɛqɛt*	SNil: distrib; phonol (*q*)	
mwok "neck"	ptSNil **muo:k* "throat"	SNil: distrib	

ORIGIN: Southern Nilotic language, probably more closely related to Kalenjin than to Dadog. Reason: words which are not common Southern Nilotic are limited to Kalenjin instead of to Dadog. But the difference between this language and Kalenjin is quite great, and so its separation from Kalenjin may be very nearly as early as Dadog's. Time of borrowing: see Chapter 6.

COMPARISON: Source language is probably closely related to the source of the loanwords of Appendix H.2. Reason: similar phonetic developments—V for Kal **Vi*; *ɔ* for Kal **a*; *u* for Kal **-uɔ*; *i* for some Kal **e*. Possibly closely related to language of loanword sets of Appendix F.1. Reason: word for "small" and word for "lion" have same particular shapes as in Appendix F.1.

VOCABULARY SOURCES:

(1) *Tepeth:* Welang'uria, about 60 years old, from Katabok, Uganda; Lochomin, about 35 years old, from Katabok; Lolem, about 25 years old, from Katabok; Alexander, about 15–16 years of age, a student at the Catholic school in Amudat, Uganda, from Moruita, Uganda.

(2) Southern Nilotic: see Appendix B.1.

Southern Nilotic Loanwords in Yaaku

YAAKU	SOUTHERN NILOTIC ATTESTATION	SOURCE	COMMENTS
kiponi "oribi"	ptKal *po:in- "bushbuck"	SNil: morphol (Nil n. pref. *ki-*)	V for Kal *V*i*; cf. H.1, "oribi"
tarawiit "impala"	ptSNil *tɛrɛwe:t	SNil: distrib	*i* for SNil *e*
repeut "hartebeest"	Dadog *ro:bæ:o:d*	SNil: morphol (SNil sec. suff. in *t*)	
kemni "cave"	ptKal *kepen	SNil: distrib	
pɔyɛk "maize"	ptSNil *pai-	SNil: distrib; morphol (SNil pl. sec. suff. in *k*). Influenced in meaning by Mas. *ɔl-paek*, but not Mas.: wrong vowel	ɔ for SNil *a*
sirimi "string of beads"	ptKal *sirim- "chain"	SNil: distrib	
anyu "fiber rope"	Pokot *a:ŋwa* "hide rope"	SNil: pattern (*u* for SNil *-ua*, as in "cloth," etc.)	*u* for SNil *-ua*, *-uɔ*; *ny* for Kal ŋ
aku "cloth"	ptSNil *a:qua "piece of cloth"	SNil: distrib; phonol (*q*)	*u* for SNil *-ua*, *-uɔ*
Yaaku "the Yaaku people"	ptSNil *(y)a:k- "hunting people"	SNil: distrib	*u* for presumed SNil *-ua*, *uɔ*
muumu "oath"	ptKal *mu:m- (preSNil)	SNil: distrib	*u* for presumed SNil *-ua*, *uɔ*
porrtet, pl. *porri* "enemy"	ptKal *po:r "to fight"; *po:rio "war, battle"	SNil: deriv (< "to fight"); also morphol? (SNil sec. suff. in *t* ?)	
rɔɔx "quiver"	Dadog *ro:qd*	?	
tiri "pot"	ptKal *ter-	SNil: distrib	*i* for SNil *e*

ORIGIN: A Southern Nilotic language, possibly somewhat more closely related to Kalenjin than to Dadog. Reason: more of the words are limited to Kalenjin than are limited to Dadog. But if the language was closer to Kalenjin, it may have been only slightly so.

COMPARISON: See Appendix H.1.

VOCABULARY SOURCES:

(1)   *Yaaku:* Lepeitan Ole Lolseli, about 65 or 70 years of age, and Njokilay Ole Supuko, about 60 years old, both of DonDol, Kenya.

(2)   Southern Nilotic: see Appendix B.1.

H.3

Words Peculiar to Dadog and Akie

DADOG ATTESTATION	AKIE ATTESTATION
ma:sa:nue:d "razor"	*mɛcɛ:nwɛ:*
maqasd "honey sack"	*makata*, pl. *makaswe*
gidgido:d "very small tick"	*kɪtɪkɪt*

VOCABULARY SOURCES:
    (1) *Dadog:* see Appendix B.1.
    (2) *Akie:* see Appendix B.1.

186

Bantu Loanwords in Luo

Luo	Bantu Attestation	Source	Comments
tɪga "giraffe"	ptEVicB *-tiiga*	Bantu: distrib	
dɛdɛ "grasshopper"	Southern, east central Bantu *-teete*, ptLuhyia-Gishu *liteete*	Bantu: distrib	*d* for B *t*; B pref. *li-* > φ before *t*
maugo "tsetse fly"	ptEVicB *-bugo*	Bantu: distrib; morphol (B pref. *ma-*)	B *b* > φ (*w*)
ɔgɔŋglɔ "centipede"	General Bantu *-gongolo* "millipede"; ptEVicB "centipede"	Bantu: distrib. EVicB: specif. meaning	*l* for B *l*
ɔtɛgɔ "trap"	ptB *-teg-* "to trap"; widespread Bantu *mutego* "trap"	Bantu: distrib	B pref. *mu-* > φ
mtaragwɪ "juniper"	Buk. *kumutarakwe*	Bantu: morphol (B pref. *m(u)-*)	*mu* for Buk. *kumu-*
lupɔ "to fish"	ptB *-lub-/-lob-*	Bantu: distrib	*l* for B *l*
ngɛsɔ "small, curved knife"	ptEVicB *-geso*	Bantu: distrib; morphol (B pref. *n-*); deriv (< ptEVicB *-ges-* "to harvest")	
dala "homestead"	EasternB *-tala*; ptLuhyia-Gishu *litala*	Bantu: distrib	*l* for B *l*; *d* for B *t*; B pref. *li* > φ before *t*
olalo "bridge"	ptB *-lalo*	Bantu: distrib	*l* for B *l*
mnaye "riddle"	Buk. *kumunai*	Bantu: morphol (B pref. *mu* = *m*)	*mu* for Buk. *kumu-*

Luo	Bantu Attestation	Source	Comments
sigana "story"	ptB *-gan-* "to tell tale"; *-gano* "tale"	Bantu: distrib; morphol (B pref. *ki = si*); deriv	*si* for B pref. **ki-*
kɪŋɔ "to bewitch"	ptEVicB *-king-* "to work magic"	Bantu: distrib	
muofu "blind person"	ptB *-pokû*; ptLuhyia-Gishu **mupokû*; Buk. *omubofu*	Bantu: distrib; phonol (B sound change *kû > fu*); morphol (B pref. *mu-*)	*fu* for B **kû*; B **p > φ*
luanda "stone"	ptLuhyia-Gishu **luanda*	Bantu: morphol (B pref. *lu-*)	*l* for B **l*

ORIGIN: A Luhyia dialect. Reasons: (1) pattern of Bantu attestation—all the words are found in Luhyia dialects, and, if any of the words are limited to just a few Bantu dialects, these few dialects are always Luhyia; (2) phonological developments in the Bantu loanwords are the same as in Luhyia-Gishu, not as in other Bantu languages of the same region.

SPECIAL POINTS: Only a selection of the Luhyia loanwords in Kenya Luo have been given in this appendix, because the Luo evidence does not have direct bearing on Southern Nilotic history. The purpose of the appendix is to show the appearance of a heavy word-borrowing period in a language's vocabulary. To this end the loanwords listed have been chosen from a wide range of vocabulary. They include culture words rarely borrowed in East Africa, such as "to fish," "story," "to bewitch," and "homestead," and at least one basic word, "stone." But many other such Luhyia loanwords in Luo could be cited.

VOCABULARY SOURCES:
(1) *Luo:* Lucia Odera, about 20 years of age, a student at University College, Nairobi, of North Gem, Kenya.
(2) Bantu: see Appendix D.1.

H.5

Dadog Loanwords in Sandawe

SANDAWE	SOUTHERN NILOTIC ATTESTATION	SOURCE
sagada "group hunt"	Dadog *šæ gæ:d* "to hunt" (ptSNil *l^yɔkɔ:t*)	SNil: distrib. Dadog: phonol (*s* for Dadog *š* < *l^y*)
kiramboda "wad of tobacco"	Dadog *kiramboda*	Dadog: morphol (SNil sec. suff. in *t*)
omi "red-brown"	ptSNil *o:m-*	SNil: distrib
xola "(black-and-white ?) patched"	Dadog -*qo:l* "black-and-white patched"	Dadog: phonol (*q*)
lonka a kind of shield	ptSNil *lo:ŋ-* "shield"	SNil: distrib
somik- "three"	ptSNil *somok*; Dadog *samagu*	SNil: distrib. *Not* Dadog: specif. shape
kho "house"	ptSNil *$qɔ$*	SNil: distrib

ORIGIN: A number of the words are specifically from Dadog. A few (e.g., "three") are not from Dadog at all but rather derive from some other Southern Nilotic language and are presumably very old loans, perhaps from the same language which has left loanwords in west central Tanzanian Bantu languages (see Appendix D.8).

VOCABULARY SOURCES:
    (1) *Dadog* and Southern Nilotic: see Appendix B.1.
    (2) *Sandawe*: Otto Dempwolff, *Die Sandawe: Linguistisches und ethnographisches Material aus Deutsch-Ostafrika* (Hamburg: L. Friederichsen & Co., 1916).

H.6

Dadog Loanwords in Hatsa

Hatsa	Dadog Attestation	Source	Comments
samaka- "three"	samag- (ptSNil *somok)	SNil: distrib. Dadog specif. shape	
nyaodako "cat"	nyao:d	Dadog: morphol (Dadog sec. suff. in d)	-ko is Hatsa gender suff.
margwegapi "honey beer"	margwe:g "millet beer"	Dadog: phonol (Dadog sound change $gw < *w$); morphol (Dadog sec. suff. in g)	-pi is Hatsa gender suff.

ORIGIN: A Dadog dialect.

LANGUAGE SOURCES:

(1) *Dadog* and other Southern Nilotic: see Appendix B.1.
(2) *Hatsa:* Otto Dempwolff, "Beiträge zur Kenntnis der Sprachen in Deutsch-Ostafrika: 12. Wörter der Hatzasprache," *Zeitschrift für Kolonialsprachen*, VII (1916–17), 319–25.

BIBLIOGRAPHY

NOTE TO THE BIBLIOGRAPHY

The published materials germane to this study of Southern Nilotic history have been listed under three heads according to the manners in which the sources were used.

Under "Methodology and Theory" are works which present the basic theory and techniques for utilizing linguistic and ethnographic evidence. Of these, Meillet's book is the classic presentation of the comparative methods of historical linguistics; Sapir's monograph is still the best and most complete study of the methods of establishing time depth in a cultural history from ethnographic and linguistic evidence.

Under "Vocabulary Sources" are listed books and articles which provided vocabulary evidence supplementary to that collected by the writer. The works by Tucker, Benson, Dempwolff, and Whiteley are in general reliable and give an adequate phonological representation of their evidence. The works by Moreno, Reinisch, Bell, and Hodson are also good sources. The remaining sources are all by people without proper linguistic training and show this lack to lesser and greater extents. Some, such as the Maguire and Hobley sources, record some of their word entries corruptly; but most of the remaining sources record their evidence consistently, although they fail to notice important phonological distinctions, such as vowel length and tone.

Under "Other Sources" are listed the main ethnographies and linguistic, archaeological, and historical studies which provided the background for the understanding and handling of the vocabulary evidence for Southern Nilotic history. Most of the ethnographies are either of relatively high quality or are the only general sources available on the cultures of certain peoples. Murdock's book is included because it is the only attempt at constructing all of African culture history from ethnographic, linguistic, and other nondocumentary evidence and because it includes important sections on aspects of East African history.

I. Methodology and Theory

BLOOMFIELD, LEONARD. *Language*, Chapter 18. New York: Henry Holt & Co., 1933.

GREENBERG, J. H. "Linguistic Evidence for the Influence of the Kanuri on the Hausa." *Journal of African History*, I (1960), 205–12.

HAUGEN, EINAR. *Bilingualism in the Americas: A Bibliography and Research Guide*. University, Ala.: University of Alabama Press, 1956.

HENDERSON, EUGENIE J. A. "The Phonology of Loanwords in Some Southeast Asian Languages." *Transactions of the Philological Society*, 1951, 131–58.

HOENIGSWALD, HENRY M. *Language Change and Linguistic Reconstruction*. Chicago: University of Chicago Press, 1960.

MEILLET, ANTOINE. *La Méthode comparative en linguistique historique.* Cambridge: Harvard University Press, 1925.

SAPIR, EDWARD. *Time Perspective in Aboriginal American Culture.* Ottawa: Government Printing Bureau, 1916.

WEINREICH, URIEL. *Languages in Contact.* New York: Linguistic Circle of New York, 1953.

II. Vocabulary Sources

BARTON, JUXON. "Turkana Grammatical Notes and Vocabulary." *Bulletin of the School of Oriental and African Studies*, II (1921), 43–73.

BELL, CHRISTOPHER R. V. *The Somali Language.* London: Longmans, Green & Co., 1953.

BENSON, T. G. *Kikuyu-English Dictionary.* Oxford: Clarendon Press, 1964.

DEMPWOLFF, OTTO. "Beiträge zur Kenntnis der Sprachen in Deutsch-Ostafrika: 4. Kulia." *Zeitschrift für Kolonialsprachen*, V (1914–15), 26–44, 113–36.

———. *Die Sandawe: Linguistisches und ethnographisches Material aus Deutsch-Ostafrika.* Hamburg: L. Friederichsen & Co., 1916.

HILDERS, J. H., and J. C. D. LAWRENCE. *An English-Ateso and Ateso-English Vocabulary.* Kampala: Eagle Press, 1958.

HOBLEY, C. W. "Further Notes on the El Dorobo or Oggiek." *Man*, V (1905), 39–44.

HODSON, ARNOLD W., and CRAVEN H. WALKER. *Elementary and Practical Grammar of the Galla or Oromo Language.* London: Society for Promoting Christian Knowledge, 1922.

HOHENBERGER, JOHANNES. *Semitisches und hamitisches Sprachgut im Masai.* Sachsenmühle: Privately printed, 1958.

HOLLIS, A. C. *The Nandi: Their Language and Folklore.* Oxford: Clarendon Press, 1909.

HUNTINGFORD, G. W. B. "Modern Hunters: Some Account of the Kamelilo-Kapchepkendi Dorobo (Okiek) of Kenya Colony." *Journal of the Royal Anthropological Institute*, LIX (1929), 333–78.

MAGUIRE, R. A. "Il-Torobo: Being Some Notes on the Various Types of Dorobo Found in the Masai Reserve of Tanganyika Territory and Contiguous Districts." *Journal of the African Society*, XXVII (1928), 127–41, 249–68.

MERKER, M. *Die Masai.* Berlin: D. Reimer, 1904.

MORENO, MARTINO MARIO. *Manuale di Sidamo.* Milan: A. Mondadori, 1940.

MÜLLER, EMIL. *Wörterbuch der Djaga-Sprache (Madjame-Mundart).* Hamburg: Eckardt & Messtorff, 1947.

REINISCH, LEO. *Die Saho-Sprache.* 2 vols. Vienna: Alfred Hölder, 1889, 1890.

SWYNNERTON, G. H. "Vernacular Names of Some of the Better-Known Mammals in the Central Province, Tanganyika." *Tanganyika Notes and Records*, No. 21 (1946), 21–38.

TUCKER, A. N., and JOHN TOMPO OLE MPAAYEI. *A Masai Grammar with Vocabulary*. London: Longmans, Green & Co., 1955.

———— and M. A. BRYAN. "Noun-Classification in Kalenjin: Nandi-Kipsigis." *African Language Studies*, V (1964), 192–247; VI (1965), 117–87.

————. "Noun-Classification in Kalenjin: Päkot." *African Language Studies*, III (1962), 137–81.

WHITELEY, W. H. *A Short Description of Item Categories in Iraqw*. Kampala: East African Institute of Social Research, 1958.

III. Other Sources

BUTT, AUDREY. *The Nilotes of the Anglo-Egyptian Sudan and Uganda*. London: International African Institute, 1952.

CERULLI, ERNESTA. *Peoples of South-West Ethiopia and Its Borderland*. London: International African Institute, 1956.

COLE, SONIA. *The Prehistory of East Africa*. London: George Weidenfeld & Nicolson, 1963.

FAGAN, BRIAN M. "Radiocarbon Dates for Sub-Saharan Africa—I." *Journal of African History*, II (1961), 137–39.

————. "Radiocarbon Dates for Sub-Saharan Africa—V." *Journal of African History*, VIII (1967), 513–27.

FLEMING, HAROLD. "Baiso and Rendille: Somali Outliers." *Rassegna di Studi Etiopici*, XX (1964), 35–96.

GRAY, ROBERT F. *The Sonjo of Tanganyika*. London: Oxford University Press, 1963.

GREENBERG, J. H. *The Languages of Africa*. Bloomington: Indiana University Research Center in Anthropology, Folklore, and Linguistics, 1963.

————. "Nilotic, 'Nilo-Hamitic' and Hamito-Semitic: A Reply." *Africa*, XXVII (1957), 364–78.

GULLIVER, PAMELA, and PHILIP H. GULLIVER. *The Central Nilo-Hamites*. London: International African Institute, 1953.

HUNTINGFORD, G. W. B. "The Economic Life of the Dorobo." *Anthropos*, XLIX (1954), 602–34.

————. *The Galla of Ethiopia; the Kingdoms of Kafa and Janjero*. London: International African Institute, 1955.

————. *The Nandi of Kenya*. London: Routledge & Kegan Paul, 1953.

————. *The Northern Nilo-Hamites*. London: International African Institute, 1953.

————. "The Political Organization of the Dorobo." *Anthropos*, XLIX (1949), 123–48.

―――. "The Social Institutions of the Dorobo." *Anthropos*, XLVI (1951), 1–48.

―――. *The Southern Nilo-Hamites*. London: International African Institute, 1953.

KÖHLER, OSWIN. *Geschichte der Erforschung der Nilotischen Sprachen*. Berlin: Reimer, 1955.

LA FONTAINE, J. S. *The Gisu of Uganda*. London: International African Institute, 1959.

LAWRENCE, J. C. D. *The Iteso*. Oxford University Press, 1957.

LEWIS, HERBERT. "The Origins of the Galla and Somali." *Journal of African History*, VII (1966), 27–46.

LEWIS, I. M. *Peoples of the Horn of Africa: Somali, Afar and Saho*. London: International African Institute, 1955.

MURDOCK, GEORGE PETER. *Africa: Its Peoples and Their Culture History*. New York: McGraw-Hill Book Co., 1959.

OGOT, B. A. *History of the Southern Luo*, Vol. I. Nairobi: East African Publishing House, 1967.

PERISTIANY, J. G. *The Social Institutions of the Kipsigis*. London: G. Routledge & Sons, 1939.

PRINS, A. H. J. *East African Age-Class Systems*. Groningen: J. B. Wolters, 1953.

RUEL, M. J. "Kuria Generation Classes." *Africa*, XXXII (1962), 14–36.

SUTTON, J. E. G. "The Archeology and Early Peoples of the Highlands of Kenya and Northern Tanzania." *Azania*, I (1966), 37–57.

WAGNER, GÜNTER. *The Bantu of North Kavirondo*. 2 vols. London: Oxford University Press, 1949.

WERE, GIDEON S. *A History of the Abaluyia of Western Kenya*. Nairobi: East African Publishing House, 1967.

WILSON, G. McL. "The Tatoga of Tanganyika." *Tanganyika Notes and Record's* No. 33 (1952), 34–47; No. 34 (1953), 35–56.

INDEX

Afar, 32n
Akie (Mosiro), 6, 8, 12, 14, 23, 28, 55, 68n, 74, 75, 94, 105, 107, 113, 126, 161, 168, 186
Alagwa, 39n, 58, 115
Aramanik, 39n, 45, 55, 56, 74, 76, 77, 115, 124, 126, 127
Arbore, 110

Bahr al-Ghazal, 35
Baiso, 32n, 110
Barabaig, 3, 6, 8, 61, 113
Baraguyu, 76
Bari, 10n
Bonde, 161
Bukusu, 8, 18, 68, 69, 131, 145, 147–49, 154, 158–60, 187
Bungoma, 68
Burun, 10n, 35
Burungi, 39n, 56n, 58, 114, 115, 117, 119, 121

Central Sudanic peoples, 35n
Chaga, 54, 71n, 138
Cherangany Range, 66

Dadog, 3, 6, 8, 12, 14–16, 19, 20, 22, 27–29, 43, 47, 50, 51, 53, 55–62, 74, 81, 83, 85, 94–99, 107, 110–15, 120, 121, 124, 125, 130, 132, 134, 135, 139, 141, 143, 144, 150–52, 156, 162, 164, 172, 183–86, 189, 190
Dahalo, 115, 122
Dinka, 10n, 35, 95
Dorobo, 6, 8, 12, 23, 38, 66, 68n, 72, 73, 75, 106

East Kalenjin, 12, 68, 72, 73, 76, 106, 107, 113, 154, 176, 177
East Rift Southern Cushitic, 122
East Victoria Bantu, 42, 44n, 130, 131, 156, 157, 159, 160, 187, 188
Eastern Cushites/Eastern Cushitic, xi, xii, 32–34, 36, 38, 78, 79, 96, 110–13
Eastern highlands of Kenya, 80, 83
Eastern Nilotes/Eastern Nilotic, xi–xiii, 10, 15n, 35, 38, 39, 47, 48, 81, 85, 92, 107
Eastern Sudan region, 34, 78
Eldama, 72
Elgon Kalenjin, 8, 12, 13n, 66, 68, 70, 113
Ethiopian highlands, 33, 35, 36, 78

Galla, 32n, 33, 110–13
Ganda, 71n, 160
Geleba, 32n, 111
Gishu, 8, 20, 42, 50, 68, 145
Gogo, 44
Gorowa, 22, 58, 60, 125
Gudella, 32n
Gusii, 24, 38, 55, 63, 71, 119, 131–35, 153, 160
Gweno, 54

Hamites/Hamitic, xi, 38, 78
Hatsa, 125, 190
Hehe, 143

Idakho, 8, 71, 131, 145, 146, 157, 158
Iramba, 59
Irangi, 58
Iraqw, 6, 19, 22, 39n, 45, 55, 58–60, 114–21, 125